Dog Hearted

Dog Hearted

Essays on Our Fierce and Familiar Companions

**Edited by Rowan Hisayo Buchanan
and Jessica J. Lee**

DAUNT BOOKS

First published in the United Kingdom in 2023 by
Daunt Books
83 Marylebone High Street
London W1U 4QW

1

A CIP catalogue record for this title is available from the British Library.

ISBN 978–1–914198–27–4

Typeset by Marsha Swan

Printed and bound by TJ Books Limited, Padstow, Cornwall

www.dauntbookspublishing.co.uk

Contents

Introduction

*Rowan Hisayo Buchanan
and Jessica J. Lee*

Dogs are the family we choose. They are dirty and toothy, but we let them into our homes and onto our beds.

It will come as no surprise to readers that this anthology sprang to life during a dog walk. All winter, we walked our two dogs around various London parks, trying to discuss writing but more often wrangling our misbehaving hounds. So while one dog tried to chew things he shouldn't and the other tried to chase dogs five times her size, we fell into talking about what these wild, familiar creatures meant to us. As writers working in often vastly different genres, we both found our relationship with dogs strangely evocative. Dogs leap across genre barriers, dragging along with them questions about what it means to own, to care for, to outlive and to love creatures with whom we only ever share a fractured language.

We've named this collection after a line from *King Lear*. Regan and Goneril, Lear's ungrateful, fake, fawning daughters, are described as 'dog-hearted'. It's an insult. Like two lapdogs, they have simpered for treats from their father, only to effectively bite his hand now that they have his kingdom. It's not the most flattering comparison for poor canines. It's also a strange insult given that dogs have long been symbols of loyalty, their small curled forms carved into the bottoms of tombs. Yet we enjoy the ambivalence. Greyfriars Bobby may have spent fourteen years guarding his master's tomb, and Hachiko may have spent nine years by a train station waiting for his master to get off the train, but they didn't have to. When we play with our dogs – a game of tug or fetch – they open their mouths to show all of their teeth. They never bite. But the teeth say, *I could.*

When we talked to other writers about their dogs, we learned that to them, too, dogs were more than cute tails and wet noses. The fourteen essays that follow consider *Canis familiaris* in all their fealty and ferocity: from the wild other to the best friend, to dogs lost and longed for. These essays explore how the ecologies of our daily lives are transformed by their companionship, and how dogs confront us with our own animality.

A few themes emerged unbidden as the essays came together, some more obvious than others. Readers may not be surprised to find essays here that explore growing families and companion-ship. For Nell Stevens and Eley Williams, dog ownership brings a new love language to family life, while Jessica Pan makes efforts to convince her husband that dogs are, indeed, as great as she (and we!) think they are. In Ned Beauman's comic essay, being a grown man with a pint-sized, child-enthralling Havanese leads him to question how others may perceive him – and what they may make of his intentions.

Dogs invite us to consider the canine legacies of the cities we inhabit, as historian Chris Pearson does, or, as Nina Mingya Powles shows, they crystallise the ways we long for places we've left behind. We (Rowan and Jessica) found ourselves examining different aspects of the underdog or runt, while Sharlene Teo – trawling for memes as much as memories – takes solace in dogs better left online.

There are dogs that sustain and guide us in our darker moments, and dogs we sustain as they reach their last days. alice hiller, processing the trauma of sexual abuse, dwells in the reassuring presence of her rescue dog. Cal Flyn finds herself tamed by an ageing retired sled dog, and Esmé Weijun Wang finds quietude in the simple act of observing her dog Daphne.

In some essays, rule-breakers run circles around their owners. Evie Wyld reminds us that when it comes to dogs, there are fiercer, bloodier notions than companionship afoot. Carl Phillips asks how wildness is tamed. And ought we to – *can we even* – tame it?

Amidst the good, 'bad', strayed and idealised dogs of this collection, you may encounter a dog like your own. Or maybe not. They are, after all, their own creatures, each dog as particular as us.

A Note on the Illustrations

The illustrations in this book are by Rowan, with the exception of those in Esmé Weijun Wang's essay. The writers sent Rowan photos of their dogs for reference, sometimes these were fresh snaps and others were photos of photos: records of dogs long past. As she inked, she was struck by the variety of size and expression within this motley pack. She hopes you enjoy meeting them.

Dog Hearted

Essays on Our Fierce
and Familiar Companions

Table Scraps

Cal Flyn

When I met Suka for the first time, she was working as a sled dog in the north of Finland. I was working there too.

It was a hard, physical lifestyle, but it had its consolations. The dogs began to howl for their breakfast at four or five in the morning, as we lugged heavy sledges laden with meat through the dark. I didn't see daylight for more than a month, but the sky was a shifting wall of technicolour: a pink and purple dawn teasing the sky for hours, never quite spilling into sunrise. Blood-red noons. The moon hung heavy in the sky, burnt orange, and at night, the stars blazed with a fierce intensity. The aurora in veils of green and gold.

This was the winter of 2012. I'd taken the kennels job as an escape route from a life in the city that had been making me sick. What had begun as urban ennui had metastasised into a more malignant form of depression, one I had never experienced before. By the time I left London for the Arctic, I'd had the uncanny sensation of watching my life unfold as if through glass for a period of six months or more.

I'd known instinctively that the harshness of an Arctic climate and a challenging manual job would serve as a sort of shock therapy for my brain: that through corporeal trial I might reunite body and mind, force them to work in concert once more. So there I was, in Finland, shovelling shit in the snow, in exchange for food and board. As a career move, I wouldn't recommend it. But the thing is: it worked.

My soft hands coarsened – I grew callouses on my palms and my numb fingertips were peeling. My sinews tightened, my clavicles sharpened. I felt more fully alive than I had in years.

To begin with, the dogs were an anonymous canine horde with deep barks and flashing eyes. But soon I saw them for who they really were: good-natured familiars, with names and personalities. Monty, the old boy with only half a tongue – an injury from licking ice-cold metal as a pup. Pikkis, with his big black eyes and phocine face. Little Rosie, who would jump from the roof of her kennel into your outstretched arms. And Suka.

Suka was my favourite dog: a docile, heart-faced creature who closed her eyes in ecstasy when you rubbed her rump. Small in stature and not too strong, she might not have been a valuable sled dog had she not been the only female dog submissive enough to run with Hulda – an athletic, pointy-eared bitch – without getting into fights. Designing dog teams is a feat of matchmaking: the dogs run in pairs, sorted for strength and intelligence. Everyone has to get along with their partners. As long as Hulda was running, Suka had an impor-tant role: official wing-woman to the top female lead dog. I liked to watch them together on the start line: Hulda snapping and yowling, cavorting like a demon in her harness, ready to run. Suka beside her, ears perked, waiting, sweet-natured.

When she was allowed in at night, I would bribe her to sleep on my bed, curled up tight like a cat. Where the other dogs were bouncy or rambunc-tious, she was watchful and reserved. She was, in other words, a perfect companion. Whether she felt the same about me was more difficult to tell.

*

Seven years later, I am deep in concentration on a writing residency in Switzerland when I get an unexpected call from Finland. Suka is nearly eleven, ready to retire. She's slowing down, getting stiff, holding up the team. Might I give her a home? I don't hesitate.

A former colleague brings Suka overland to the UK for me. I meet them in a cafe, buy her breakfast, then it's just me and my dog. She is smaller than I remembered, and – mid-moult – has a dishevelled, bewildered air. Having barely left home for her entire life, she has travelled through five countries in as many days. My presence seems barely to register; she lets me pat her but refuses to meet my eye.

I drive us home, to where my partner Rich is waiting. We show Suka her new bed, her new bowls, her new collar. We take her for a sniff around the town. People want to know: *Did she recognise you?* I say it's difficult to tell.

It's difficult to tell a lot of things. Suka is quiet and respectful. She gets up when I ask her to. Sits when I tell her to. She'll take a treat gently from my hand, but she won't always eat it. The closest comparison I can find is that it's like hosting a foreign exchange student; she is scrupulously, unfailingly polite. But I have the very faintest impression she might be saving up slights to tell her friends about later.

On our first walks, she finds a cold welcome from the local dogs. Something in her gait, her manner – her smell, perhaps – seems to get their backs up. She assumes a dignified bearing, declines to engage. When, finally, a friendly pup approaches, almost frantic to meet her, Suka doesn't seem to know how to react. Out of a hundred huskies she might have been the softest of them all, but here amid the Labradors and spaniels, she seems proud and stand-offish.

In the house, I don't quite know how to place her. She does not follow me around, as other dogs will. She has her own agenda. She does not beg at the table. She does not bark. She does not come when she is called.

Her body language is peculiar too. She will wag her tail, but the exact meaning is difficult to parse: rather than the uncomplicated happiness of a pet dog getting its cuddles, it signals a more ambiguous kind of anticipation. Praise or attention might merit a slow pendulum swing, but the approach of an aggressive dog or a visit to the vet occasionally elicits a fulsome swish of the kind I might once have hoped for on arriving home after a long day.

She is entirely benevolent, except when she's not. She has no interest in fighting. She is entirely neutral on the subject of cats. But early one morning, in the dancing light of a sun cast low through bare branches, a sparrow darts from a tumbledown wall and her jaws snap shut. It leaves this world as fast as it appeared. She swallows it whole. This makes me look at her afresh: this dog knows what she's doing.

It's not that I'm unnerved, or not exactly. She's still the calm and passive creature I fell in love with. But I begin to see her in new light. There's the faintest thread of menace running through her, an undercurrent of cool self-interest. As it must, of course, in every dog – no matter how small, how cute, how apparently frivolous. It's just that, in Suka, the wolf runs closer to the surface than I'd known.

Less than a month after her arrival, Suka falls deathly ill. It's an acute uterine infection, of an urgency and seriousness equivalent to appendicitis in humans. One evening she seems a bit peaky; the next morning she can barely stand. We rush her into emergency surgery, and by the time she returns to us, days later, she is glassy-eyed and missing her womb. She has stitches in her belly.

For the first few nights after her return, I sleep with her on the kitchen floor. By the third or fourth, she sleeps with me on my mat, curled into the recess between my legs and belly, not quite touching me but close. I feel ill with relief. Sickeningly, painfully grateful. And more: it feels like something has shifted between us. She knows who I am to her now, if not who I was before. There is warmth, where before there was only tolerance. But, as she recovers, something else is changing too: a kind of reshuffling is underway, our positions in the social hierarchy are evolving.

In Finland, I was her boss and I treated her – and her kennel mates – accordingly. I ordered them to step back as I opened the door. I caught them quickly, even roughly. Harnessed them. Brooked no objections. There were strict boundaries and she respected them. They all did. Now, in our shared house, the balance has shifted. We are all adults here, cohabiting. Negotiating.

It no longer feels reasonable to force my will on her. She's retired; I'm a self-employed writer. There is no hard schedule to adhere to. It seems important that our life together is based on mutual consent. If she's hungry, I feed her. If she's restless, I walk her. *She doesn't ask for much,* I say to Rich. And it's true. But the truth is, I would give anything to please her. Anything at all.

Her presence reveals certain weaknesses in my character I haven't previously confronted. I find myself desperate for her approval, flushing with jealousy if she shows even the faintest preference for certain friends or neighbours. In the face of her nonchalance, I am needier than I have ever been in love. I clamour for her attentions, debase myself for her affection daily. When she's fired up, I'll get down on all fours to prance with her. When she howls to the sky, I will howl in answer. I have lost all self-consciousness in pursuit of her approval. What can I do to make her love me the way that I love her?

I pore over guides to canine behaviour, in search of a self-help philosophy. I read somewhere that for a dog to respect you, one should train them, have them do your bidding. Suka knows how to sit and lie down on command, and she will – but when she obeys I feel she does so with a sense of irony. I teach her to 'stay', and to offer her paw. She considers my requests sceptically, and more often declines. In exchange, I offer titbits, but she does not always take them. She is not, as they say, 'food-motivated'. Nor is she stirred by praise. She would not be so basic. Suka is powered by some internal fire that burns untended by you or me.

In fact, food soon becomes our greatest source of anxiety. She never quite regains her appetite after her illness. She picks over her food, turns her nose up at the rest. She loses weight, becomes rangy and ragged. Panicked, I take up a new role as kitchen maid, cooking scrambled eggs at a few hours' interval. I shred chicken breasts into bone broth. Grate parmesan over raw beef. I follow her from room to room offering dainty morsels served straight from my fingertips.

I am not unaware of my descent. Occasionally I voice faint misgivings to the vet: *might we have passed from the pathological into preciousness? Am I creating a monster?* The verdict is always the same: *Perhaps, yes.* But they point to her free-falling weight, her erratic health. What's more important? My pride, my dignity? Or keeping her alive?

I'm keeping her alive. God willing, she will turn fourteen this year. In return, I accept my fallen status. With time, our roles have solidified. She has adopted the regal air of an ageing monarch whose body is slowly failing her. I am her devoted hand-maiden, bowing and scraping. When she walks, we move down the street in stately, slow-moving caval-cade, stopping when she wants to stop – to read messages on a nearby lamp post, perhaps, or to greet her loyal subjects – and turning back when she tires of the whole production.

When she first arrived, I expected her to soften, to relax into the character of the panting lapdog. To prostrate herself on rugs, upturn her belly for rubs. And though it's true that as she grows older, she deigns more often than ever to express her favour – leaning into me while I rub her neck, tucking her head under my arm, table scraps of understated affection just enough to keep me going – she has in many ways grown harder, more private, ever more imperial in response to my endless adulation.

Suka's strength fluctuates, but the trend is downhill. We slalom with her. Such is the agony of dog ownership: the way our timers draw down in asynchrony. It's hard to accept her sand might be running out. Despite her self-possession, Suka – born in a kennel to run in a team – doesn't really like to be alone. I can't bear to think of her taking that last walk through the dark without me.

When she is feeling ill, there is one fail-safe trick to lift her from her starvation diet. A little fresh blood, drunk straight from the bowl, or drizzled over rice, or frozen into cubes. When I pour it out, I see awareness pass through her. Her nostrils will flair, her muzzle will lift. I see a tightening around the eyes, as the room comes into focus. A flicker of the wolf that lives inside her still.

Not yet. Each day we fend off death, one morsel at a time. It's blood she wants. It's blood she needs. But it is me who, now she is old and tired, walks down to the butcher and begs for it.

Walking Through the Past and Present with Cassie

Chris Pearson

8.40 a.m. Friday 11 February 2022. The kids have just left the house to go to school and it's time for me to take Cassie for her morning walk. Cassie is a nine-month-old Bedlington whippet puppy. In other words, she's a lurcher. Richard II of England banned commoners from owning greyhounds in 1389, and so non-elite hunters bred lurchers for hunting and poaching. Down the centuries, the lurcher's skill and intelligence became almost mythical. 'If half the stories told of the docility and intelligence of the lurcher are true, the poacher needs no other help than one of these dogs for ground game,' noted one Victorian commentator, five hundred years after Richard II's decree.[1] Cassie certainly has the lurcher docility: most often she has to be dragged from the sofa to go for a walk.

Cassie's hunting skills remain untested. But when she's not lounging on her bed or sofa, she is a lively presence in the house and always on the lookout for cuddles, attention and food. She is one of the many puppies bought during the interminable Covid-19 pandemic and she has certainly brightened up the WFH situation and life in general. Since the fraught early days of house-training her and trying to restrain her nips and jumping, she has slotted almost seamlessly into our lives. People often say that dogs live in the present and so help keep you in the moment too. In my experience, there is much truth in this. But as an historian who has worked on human–canine histories for the last ten years, I know that the bonds between Cassie and I are deeply historical. When I walk Cassie, I'm walking in the past and present.

We leave our house, a late Victorian/early Edwardian red-brick terrace in Chester. By the time the house was built, the Victorian middle-class cult of domesticity had enveloped dogs. Countless dog care books – some funded by Spratt's and other newly established dog food companies – explained to middle-class Victorians how to make dogs part of the family. Trained, groomed and well-fed dogs entered middle-class homes and propped up cultural values and emotional norms that prized sentimentality, cleanliness and the home as a comfortable refuge from the harsh outside world. Here was a love and tenderness that could be celebrated. When not writing cookery books, Harriet de Salis wrote a manual for dog keepers in which she declared that 'the love of dogs is natural to most people,' and 'I *cannot* understand how anyone can ill-treat them.'[2]

Dogs loved humans back, and the evidence for this could be found everywhere from books and newspaper articles to Darwinian science and everyday interactions. The power of canine love dovetailed with moral imperatives. 'The mission of the dog . . . is the same as the mission of Christianity, namely, to teach mankind that the universe is ruled by love. Ownership of a dog tends to soften the hard hearts of men,' observed American lawyer and writer Henry Childs Merwin.[3]

Of course, not everyone loved the ways of the Victorian dog owner. Critics frequently homed in on the deformed features of pedigree dogs, the cost of keeping dogs and the obsessiveness of their owners. One French observer of New York's dogs believed English greyhounds to be among the city's unhappiest dogs. They were kept by business-men who wanted to look the part, but these 'noble animals' were repulsed by their 'bourgeois lifestyle and commercial habits.' Such hounds were not made for the pavements and shop-filled streets of New York. Instead, they dreamed of the country-side of their 'home country.'[4] Leaving aside the distaste for American capitalism, these observa-tions are striking as – for once – a wealthy man is singled out for blame and for putting his needs above canine ones. For more often than not, male critics bemoaned the excessive love that female dog owners displayed towards their pets (invariably depicted as spoilt lapdogs), a love that would be better diverted towards their fellow humans and children. An article in *Pearson's Magazine* contrasted the miseries of New York's orphans with the luxurious lives enjoyed by the dogs of rich women. In ignoring the orphans' plight, these apparently dog-obsessed women displayed their selfishness and had turned their backs on their natural maternal instinct.[5] American neurologist Charles Loomis Dana even claimed to have discovered the zoophilic psychosis, with those affected overwhelmed by an obsessive love for animals. Women, it went without saying, were most susceptible.

Knowing these things troubles me somewhat. The Victorian cult of domesticity, with all its suffocating gender norms, is not something that I admire nor wish to reproduce. Yet Cassie *feels* like part of the family and our home is her home. She makes our home feel more like a refuge (however illusional) from the rest of the world, and we all go soppy around her. Dogs also offered constant and important companionship during the Covid-19 lockdown, especially for those living on their own.[6]

These bonds are much more than misplaced senti-mentality. As you might have guessed, my sympa-thies lie with the Victorian dog lovers rather than their critics. But I also worry that the celebration of pets like Cassie obscures other equally valid forms of human–canine companionship in which dogs are not restricted to homes, like the street dogs of Delhi or Istanbul. Ultimately, knowing that modern Western pet-keeping is rooted in Victorian homes and is therefore historical and not natural helps me remember that Cassie's place in my family's home is only one way of living with dogs.[7]

Out on the street, Cassie pulls on her lead (despite the advice from the puppy manuals, the pulling continues). The lead is a very simple piece of technology that lies at the heart of human–canine relations in the West. It connects me and Cassie and makes it obvious to passers-by that she is my dog and that I am responsible for her. It also stops her running off (despite the advice from the puppy manuals, walking to heel and recall are works-in-progress).

But walking dogs on a lead has a particular history. At the beginning of the nineteenth century, free-ranging dogs roamed cities. Some were owned and let loose during the day and others were ownerless street dogs who fed off the ample food waste and other debris strewn across the cityscape. In nineteenth-century Europe and North America, a growing chorus of public health officials, veterinarians and journalists branded street dogs dirty, dangerous and diseased, and equated them with the so-called 'dangerous classes', those members of the working class who were deemed too poor and degenerate to integrate into wider society. Like the dogs they allegedly bred and set forth to wander the streets, the dangerous classes menaced the rest of society. The Victorian cult of domesticity combined with wider fears of vagabondage and urban disorder to brand these dogs as suspect because they deviated from their designated place: the home. As British dog breeder Gordon Stables argued in 1877, 'dogs have far too much liberty. In our villages and towns they are allowed to do pretty much as they please, and go wherever they like – at least, the mongrel portion of the community may, for well-bred dogs are looked better after. They crowd our streets, then, eating garbage and filth, getting disease, and freely disseminating it.'[8] Street dogs' uncontrolled mobility became disruptive and dangerous because it impeded the free and safe circulation of humans and other animals within the city. Public hygiene concerns and fears over mobile and marginal populations – tramps and vagabonds – coalesced in depictions of street dogs.

City authorities unleashed numerous measures against street dogs: dogcatchers, poison on the streets, impoundment, death. Cities thereby became ever more dangerous places for street dogs. One of their French human defenders, for there were some, imagined a letter sent from a dog named Figaro to one of his friends, Azor, in the provinces. Having left his peaceful village to see Paris, Figaro finds himself falling 'victim' to the police prefect's ordinances and treated like a 'vile criminal'. Snatched off the street and brought to the 'hell' of the pound where 'bodies cover the floorboards', Figaro is thrown together with all kinds of innocent dogs. Figaro is about to be slaughtered when his frantic owner appears and rescues him. Advising Azor to never go to Paris, Figaro vows to return to the village as soon as he can.[9] Perhaps intended as a warning to human provincials tempted to seek their fortunes in Paris, the narrative attributed to Figaro nonetheless portrays Paris as a dangerous place for dogs in which any dog could be treated as a stray, lose its freedom and be exposed to the pound's brutality.

Fears of rabies fed the loathing of street dogs. Compared to other diseases, such as cholera, very few people died from rabies. But this was a truly horrific disease that cast doubt on the bonds between humans and dogs. Anxieties of rabies were such that doctors wondered if some patients who presented with hydrophobic symptoms might be suffering from fears of rabies rather than the disease itself. Imaginary hydrophobia was nonetheless a serious matter, especially during rabies outbreaks. Benjamin Collins Brodie, a surgeon at St George's Hospital, London, claimed that during the rabid summer of 1830 some 'patients had died of the mere terror . . . the state of anxiety in which I have seen people in over and over again, after having been bitten by strange dogs . . . a very serious evil indeed.'[10] And once the horrendous symptoms set in, death was inevitable.

Doctors published extensive case notes that outlined, in gruesome detail, the stages of the disease. Dr Henry Guernsey, a New York physician, reported the tragic case of a New Yorker bitten by a dog in September 1856. The man later tried to drink a 'glass of gin, but found it to produce a violent spasm, which warned him of his fearful condition. He knew he had Hydrophobia . . . He retired immediately to bed, and endeavored to sleep, but his restless, agitated mind prevented him . . . he was prostrated with fear, and in great agony, but without pain; he said it was indescribable.' Guernsey gathered a team of doctors to bear witness to this 'disease which triumphs over our art,' and to help him administer treatments: 'stimulants, narcotics, anodynes, and counter-irritants.' These administrations brought some relief before the patient yielded to the 'hand of the destroying angel.'[11] Such accounts made their way into the press and unsurprisingly heightened anxieties.

Pet dogs could spread rabies within the sanctum of the home: beware the 'poisoned kisses' of your beloved pooch, warned French veterinarian and rabies authority Henri Bouley, for they might spread infected saliva.[12] But – and it is hard to overexaggerate how common this view was – most blamed street dogs for spreading rabies. They were the 'principal cause' of the disease's spread, French officials noted in 1885.[13] *King Solomon's Mines* author H. Rider Haggard called for the British government to take action to avoid his children and others following the fate of David Benjamin Plummer, a nine-year-old boy who had died of rabies: 'death on the rack would be an infinitely more merciful end than death by rabies.'[14] The introduction of lethal chambers into pounds and shelters towards the end of the nineteenth century allowed dogs to be 'put to sleep' calmly and efficiently, unlike previous methods of slaughter: hanging, poisoning and drowning. By the end of the nineteenth century, and despite Louis Pasteur's feted rabies vaccination, ever-increasing numbers of street dogs were removed from European and North American cities. Colonialism spread these methods across the globe, including culls against the street dogs of Singapore in 1884–5 and Port Elizabeth, South Africa, in 1893–4 during rabies outbreaks. It seems likely that British dog owners imported the disease in their pedigree pets, but colonisers blamed local street dogs who bore the brunt of the violence.

To return to Cassie tugging at the lead. This simple means of binding dog and human together allowed dog owners to promenade with their dog through the city and protect their pet from capture, impoundment and potential death. For Western nineteenth-century anti-street dog legislation targeted the unleashed dog. Without a lead, dogs were presumed dangerous, rabid and unowned, and were moving targets for capture and death.

The nineteenth-century laws that prescribed the leashing of dogs were tightened up in the twentieth century and they are now particularly restrictive in twentieth-first century Britain in places under the sway of Public Spaces Protection Orders (formerly Dog Control Orders), such as certain parks and nature reserves.

I feel conflicted about the lead (as I do about many things). It keeps Cassie close to me and safe from cars and other dangers. But the lead is bound up in the violent removal of street dogs from Western streets. I sometimes wonder if Cassie, too, would be happier wandering as she pleases, sniffing wherever she wants and eating whatever she can find. But unless I train her *really* well – to walk, to heel – and unless we get recall perfected, the lead is here to stay and keeps us walking on the right side of the law. A loose dog – however well trained, however domesticated, however much I may care for her – is still considered a dangerous dog.

Once we've walked for a few minutes down the street and she's had her morning wee, we reach a gentle slope where the road dips downwards. More often than not, this is where Cassie starts sniffing the pavement intently and tugging even more on the lead. It's poop time. As she strains, I instinctively reach for the dog poo bags in my pocket and mutter 'good girl' once she has performed (house-training habits die hard). Even this aspect of my everyday life with Cassie has a history and accompanying legislation. The Dogs (Fouling of Land) Act 1996 and subsequent legislation requires me to 'scoop the poop' or, more accurately, pick it up with a plastic bag. Similar legislation is in effect elsewhere in the Western world, spearheaded by New York City's 'pooper scoop' law of 1978 with some cities (very often Paris) singled out as being dog mess hotspots. The thought of having to pick up dog mess once put me off keeping a dog, but now it's become an everyday (or sometimes twice or thrice a day) occurrence.

In the nineteenth century, things were somewhat different: 'pure finders' in London and Paris collected dog mess to sell to tanneries to treat leather. There was plenty of raw material for them, with street and pet dogs free to defecate where they liked. Their excrement mixed with horse manure, mud, rubbish and other sludge on the city streets. The demise of the urban horse and introduction of better street-cleaning measures around the turn of the century, though, represented a turning point, rendering dog mess a disgusting spectacle on otherwise relatively clean city streets. Doctors and public hygienists in the 1920s and 1930s highlighted the parasites and diseases that lurked within. But despite some 'Curb Your Dog' campaigns in New York and anti-fouling by-laws in London, it was not until the post-war period that councils began to take dog mess more seriously. Urban improvement societies joined the crusade. In 1940s New York the Outdoor Cleanliness Association set up a Canine Club 'run' by the dogs of the women who led the organisation (Minnie von Brannfelz, an AKC-registered dachshund belonging to Miss Sherwood, was the founder president). For 50 cents a year dogs could join the club and submit to its rules, promising to make 'a bee line for the gutter instead of loitering to sniff and read the news first.' In line with the club's aim of 'Cleanliness, Care and Consideration', its members would give demonstrations on how to use the gutter.

Health scares and disgust at dog dirt led to heightened public and press outcry in the 1970s. Burnley in northern England became a particular flashpoint when the local council banned defecating dogs from the town's parks, much to the horror of their owners. So too did Paris when

Mayor Jacques Chirac promised to tackle the much lamented state of city streets that were strewn with dog *merde*. Dog mess's disgusting presence on the streets raised questions about the place of dogs in the modern city, and seemed to undermine Western norms of cleanliness and civilisation. Dogs' daily defilement of the urban landscape and their owners' indifference became symbols of urban decay, the decline of civility, and obstacles to the creation of truly modern (i.e. ordered and clean) cities. There's 'a dirty war out on the streets' proclaimed a *Times* headline in 1991. Sue Bell, chairperson of the National Dog Warden Association, noted that 'tempers get excessively frayed . . . I have chaired three very large meetings where people have had to be physically restrained.' The solution was to install dog poo bins and encourage owners to pick up the mess: 'That's the British spirit,' asserted Bell, 'the attitude that: "If I'm doing it then everyone else is jolly well going to do it, too."'[15] But despite Bell's belief in British national character and the introduction of anti-fouling laws, dog mess remains an enervating issue, and a steaming source of complaints and consternation. Out and about every day with Cassie, I keep an eye out for 'canine visiting cards' (in the words of a Parisian councillor) to stop her sniffing it or – hello, disgust reaction – eating it.[16]

Once she's finished her business, my bagged hand reaches down to collect the stinking deposit. I am now happy to bag and bin whatever Cassie deposits on the pavement. Her waste doesn't disgust me but that left by other dogs does, and I feel annoyed that their owners haven't bothered to clean up after their pets, thereby joining the ranks of dog mess complainants. Despite their often cosseted, comfortable and controlled lives, and the anxieties about dog mess expressed over the last one hundred years, the highly domesticated Western pet dog remains an animal.

Upon returning from the walk and back inside the house, Cassie's tail starts wagging. She knows she's home and is keen to get back to her comfort zone. I take off her lead and she bounds over to her sofa, the once smart blue cushions of that have been scuffed by her nails. She settles down contented as I go upstairs and write this until it's time to take her out once again to walk through the past and present together.

NOTES

1. Richard Jefferies, *The Amateur Poacher* (Cambridge: Cambridge University Press, 2010 [1879]), 231.
2. Harriet de Salis, *Dogs: A Manual for Amateurs* (London: Longmans, Green and Co., 1893), 1.
3. Henry Childs Merwin, *Dogs and Men* (Boston and New York: Houghton Mifflin Co., 1910), 7.
4. C.N. (The Atlantic Monthly), 'Les chiens de New-York' in *Revue Britannique* vol. 6 (1873), 223.
5. 'Dogs and Rabies', *Pearson's Magazine*, December 1909, 736.
6. Maythe Seung-Won Han, 'More-than-human kinship against proximal loneliness: practising emergent multi-species care with a dog in a pandemic and beyond', *Feminist Theory* 23:1 (2022): 109–24.
7. I explore the specificity of Western dog-keeping in more detail in *Dogopolis: How Dogs and Humans Made Modern New York, London, and Paris* (Chicago: University of Chicago Press, 2021).
8. Gordon Stables, *Dogs in Their Relation to the Public: Social, Sanitary and Legal* (London: Cassell, Petter and Galpin, 1877), 11.
9. *Lettre d'un chien de Paris à un de ses amis de province sur les massacres de la rue Guénégaud* (Paris: les libraires du Palais-Royal, 1825), 5–6, 14–16.
10. *Committee to Prevent the Spreading of Canine Madness, Report, Minutes of Evidence*, House of Commons, Parliamentary Papers, 651, 1830, 26.
11. New York Academy of Medicine Library, Henry Guernsey, *Hydrophobia: A Case, with Remarks* [n.d.].
12. Henri Bouley, *Hydrophobia: Means of Avoiding its Perils and Preventing its Spread as Discussed at One of the Scientific Soirees of the Sorbonne*, trans. Alexandre Liautard (New York: Harper & Brothers, 1874 [1870]), 10–11, 13.
13. Archives de la Préfecture de police, Paris, DB 232 Conseil d'hygiène publique et de salubrité du département de

la Seine, *Rapport sur les maladies contagieuses des animaux observées en 1884 dans le département de la Seine* (Paris: Imprimerie Chaix, 1885), 5.

14. H. Rider Haggard, 'Hydrophobia', *Times*, 3 November 1885.

15. Sally Brompton, 'A Dirty War Out on the Streets', *Times*, 21 July 1990.

16. Conseil municipal de Paris, 'Compte rendu de la séance du mardi 28 décembre 1937', *Supplément au Bulletin municipal officiel de la ville de Paris*, 1 January 1938, 16.

The Master List

Jessica Pan

There is a simple test to tell whether your house is truly a home. When you arrive at your front door and put the key into the lock, you need to hear the clattering of nails on a wooden floor galloping towards the door and then be greeted by a cold nose and a soft nuzzle. No nuzzle? Not a home. No cold nose? Why even bother coming home?

I've always thought this, having grown up with Rottweilers who would not only nuzzle you but fully jump on top of you and shower you with affection on your arrival.

And I had always imagined my home as an adult would have this. How wrong I was.

*

My best friend Rachel told me that you could find true love if you just wrote down all the qualities you wanted in a partner in one long comprehensive list. She had heard this from Oprah (in her magazine, not personally). Apparently, by writing down what you really desired, you would send your wishlist out into the Universe (capital U) and the Universe would deliver it to you, like Hermes or DPD.

'You should be very specific – nothing is too frivolous. And then you just let it go,' she wrote to me in an email from Paris.

It was two o'clock in the morning in Beijing, where I was living and working, when I read this revelation.

I took this advice from Oprah, via Rachel, as gospel. I did not question how this might work or why the Universe cared so much about my so-called soulmate that it was actually taking individual orders, as if from a catalogue.

Rachel had attached her list, which was amazingly specific. It included the requirements: 'athletic but not obnoxiously so' and 'speaks more than one language' and 'should always over-respond to my text messages so that I never feel insecure.'

I had not found true love yet. I'd actually been

crushed again and again during my time in Beijing, flinging myself into romantic liaisons with whomever was most exciting, including my last relationship with a journalist who was nearly twenty years older than I was. It ended with me running out of his apartment, crying, wondering if anyone would ever love me the way I wanted to be loved.

I had never stopped to consider, even once, if the journalist had the qualities I actually wanted in a long-term partner. Maybe Oprah was right, and I needed to focus my desires.

I wrote my list quickly, leaving out nothing too trivial.

'Must like Joni Mitchell,' I wrote.

I thought about how my favourite holidays were on the beach in summertime. 'Must not sunburn easily.' The list went on:

- Nice to strangers

- Loyal

- Extremely funny

- Asks questions and is actually interested in the answers

- Good hands

- Incredibly interesting but not so interesting that I feel extremely boring in comparison

I thought about how Rachel said we could be as frivolous as we wanted. My first childhood crush was caused by an ill-fated watching of *Cocktail* and then *Top Gun* at a very impressionable age. Did I dare?

'Handsome in a way that is reminiscent of Tom Cruise.'

I thought about Tom's devotion to Scientology.

'Non-religious,' I added.

In the end, the list had forty-three items.

I hit send to Rachel. We called it our 'Master List' and then we proceeded to forget it ever existed.

One year later, the Universe delivered. Its mode of delivery was through a job vacancy. Sam, an Englishman, applied for a job I'd posted. A colleague interviewed and hired him and we ended up working directly together. I had to hand it to the Universe – it was very efficient.

Of course, I didn't know then that Sam was my Master List order, but I *did* notice he had nice hands and that he looked like Tom Cruise. He was tanned after backpacking through India. He was incredibly polite to everyone in the office.

One day we happened to be in the lift together at the end of the day. He had his headphones on, and I asked what he was listening to. It was someone called Seasick Steve and it was horrendous, but before I handed his phone back to him, I scrolled through his music collection and saw her: Joni.

I wrote to Rachel that night. 'I am going to fall in love with the new guy at work.'

It happened so fast that we were actually married before he had a chance to visit my home in Texas. And that is, of course, when I found out I had forgotten one important thing from my Master List.

*

I don't realise how bad it is until my husband Sam visits my childhood home for the first time for Thanksgiving. As soon as we come through the front door, my family dog, Max, sprints towards us – ninety-five pounds of muscle, energy and pure dumb affection. Max is a Rottweiler, so the effect is not unlike a giant black bear charging. My husband freezes.

'He's just being friendly,' I say. My husband doesn't respond, because he's too busy flattening himself against a wall.

Max jumps on me, whimpering, after not having seen me for many months. You know the sound. Cries of joy, excitement and sheer disbelief. Often,

Max is so overcome with emotion that he pees on the floor.

It is wonderful to feel so loved. It is like those videos of returning veterans being reunited with their dogs except it is me and my dog, and frankly I want to pee my pants a little bit, too.

Max quickly coats my jeans with his saliva and black fur. I bury my head into his soft neck. I hear my husband clear his throat, possibly because he is on the verge of a nervous breakdown and this is his way of letting me know.

To reassure my husband of how gentle and kind my gigantic dog is, I lie down on the floor and Max rolls onto my chest, pinning me down and covering me with kisses.

'Look, he's playing!' I shout, while my husband watches on fearfully, still braced against a wall.

'Isn't he cute? So harmless?' I ask, one side of my face entirely wedged inside Max's open jaws. 'He could kill me right now but he actively chooses *not* to! Isn't that great? Isn't that so sweet?'

My husband backs out of the room slowly.

*

I can't quite remember when I found out or how I found out, but it hit me like a ninety-five-pound Rottweiler flattening me to the floor, but without the joy and affection.

Sam did not like dogs.

I felt ill when I found out. He didn't like dogs? How? Why? HOW? WHY?

He explained that he thought they were dirty animals, as if inviting them into your home was akin to petting and cuddling the rats on the subway.

'They're always jumping on you and licking you and they eat disgusting things.' He shuddered.

I didn't know where to begin. The four dogs of my childhood were family members. We adored Tasha, Shayna, Rufus and Max. Every evening was better with a dog sleeping at your feet. All meals were more fun with a dog under the table or licking up the food a child had thrown. My family talked about dogs all the time. We pointed out different ones. We petted other people's. I'm sure we loved ours more than some family members.

'But don't you want to come home to a dog, who runs to you and jumps on you and kisses you and is so excited to see you?'

Sam shook his head vigorously no.

'Don't you just want to bury your head and nuzzle a dog's neck after a hard day?'

Sam looked at me like I was insane.

'I *am* going to have a dog someday,' I said. Sam remained silent.

I was so distressed by this revelation that as soon as I got home, I frantically searched through my emails to check my Master List. How could this guy not love dogs? What else was he missing? How could he NOT be The One?

I ran through the list: 'dark hair' and 'world traveller'. Yes and yes. But I couldn't find it. 'Must love dogs' was not on the list.

I must have just thought this request was a given, like 'drinking water' and 'wearing shoes in public' or 'is a person'. OF COURSE YOU LIKE DOGS. Who doesn't like dogs?

My one true love. Apparently.

Every time you make a deal with the Universe, it's always tricky. I should have known.

But Sam loved me the way I had always wanted to be loved – unconditionally and loyally. Could I give up on a life with dogs for him?

The first time I saw Sam pet a dog we were visiting some family friends. I knew he was petting the golden retriever because *he* knew that the family expected him to, that it would seem odd if he didn't. Because what normal, sane, loving person wouldn't want to pet a golden retriever?

You know when you see someone do something and it just doesn't look right? Like a dog roller skating? It was like that, but a man gingerly petting a dog. I wanted to jump in and say, 'soft, soft, like this' as if I was guiding an inexperienced toddler.

Still, I thought there was hope. Sam and his family had never had a dog, so he simply did not understand the magic of dogs. He had just never experienced it.

You love what you are used to, and I loved big black dogs who cocked their heads to the side when they were intrigued. Who had brown dots as eyebrows. Who slept on your feet while you watched TV or read a book. Who drooled all over you and would absolutely ruin your life if you so much as dared to begin to peel an orange.

But Sam had never had a dog, so how could he possibly know what he was missing?

'When we get a dog someday,' I'd say, baiting him, 'they don't have to sleep in our bed.'

'OF COURSE WE ARE NOT LETTING A DOG SLEEP IN OUR BED.'

'Right,' I'd say, pleased that Sam had not disputed the fact that we would someday get a dog.

It carried on this way for a few years. I'd pet nearly every dog that came our way and Sam would step aside and watch from a distance.

Then, we went to Iceland. We had to drive for several hours, park and then hike to an isolated cabin on the east coast. When we arrived I was delighted to find a chocolate Labrador named Freya in residence.

Freya was a teenager and was instantly taken with us. He followed us to our door with a giant stick and would wait outside whenever we went in our room.

Each day when Sam and I would walk towards the cliffs, Freya happily accompanied us, sniffing everything in sight, so full of energy and life. He was so soft and lovely.

At night, we would sit in front of the fire and Freya would come and rest his chin on my thigh and stare at me with big sad brown eyes, utterly besotted. It made Sam laugh and laugh.

I don't think he'd ever actually appreciated a dog and their personality before. Sam didn't even think of them as having personalities – he had seen all dogs as wild animals, unpredictable and feral.

When Freya would drop a ball in front of our feet and then shimmy backwards, whining, asking us to throw it, I could see Sam finally getting it, the thing I had been saying for years: *Dogs are people too.*

At breakfast, Freya would come over to me and I'd gently stroke his neck and he'd immediately roll onto his back and howl in sheer pleasure. Sam would laugh.

It was working.

Freya accompanied us on all our walks and greeted us every morning. At night, Freya would sleep in a big dog bed on the stairs and he would snore so loudly, his lips cartoonishly billowing out air with each breath. Sam would laugh.

It was working.

Freya was very taken with a huge plank of wood but it was so large that he wasn't able to carry it through the door. But he kept trying, smashing the plank again and again against the door frame. Sam would laugh.

It was working!

I sent Rachel a photo of Sam with Freya trotting by his side.

'Omigod,' she said. 'Is Sam actually befriending a dog?'

*

It's taken several years, but now if Sam is out without me, he takes photos of dogs he thinks I might like and sends them to me. He doesn't cuddle every dog in the park, but he can appreciate them.

We don't have a dog yet because we live in a small flat in London with no garden, but it's unspoken that someday, we will, indeed, have a dog of our own.

Sam and I have a baby boy and I see raising the baby as a continuation of his education on how to love dogs. When the baby crawls around our feet, I say, 'This is exactly like having a dog.' When the baby nuzzles into us and we feel so cosy and safe, I say, 'This is exactly like having a dog.' I feel that the more he hears it, the more it will sink in, like hypnosis.

Despite the lack of clattering nails towards our door or furry nuzzles, the home Sam and I share is a home. Maybe we don't have dogs, but knowing that we someday will, well, that's enough for now.

And so, maybe my one true love did not originally love *my* true love. Yes, I had always imagined marrying a fellow dog lover, but I think this is even better. I have converted a non-believer.

At the park this week, Sam walks ahead of me, holding the hand of our baby who just started walking with all the grace of a drunk sailor looking for a fight. The baby is in a red jumpsuit made out of such puffy material that he moves like the Michelin Man. He has a massive grin on his face because he has spotted a dog. He doesn't yet have a word for dogs – instead he quivers with glee when he sees one, akin to a horse neighing in delight.

My work is almost complete. I watch as a French bulldog puppy approaches our baby. My baby neighs and my husband kneels down next to him and the dog. As my son reaches his chubby hand towards the puppy, my husband guides him and says, 'Soft, soft. Like this.'

Runt

Rowan Hisayo Buchanan

When I was sixteen, a friend made me promise I'd live to twenty-two. Things had happened that made me feel that I did not have some essential quality required for living. I thought I was lying when I said yes. But I write this in my thirties. My hands are bonier and my face more freckled and I am still alive.

Still, at sixteen, a year when I did my best to die, I also tried to save a life. I have replayed the day enough times that I feel as though I'm watching from the outside. I'll tell it like a story. I must warn you – more than one dog dies.

Here goes:

Once upon a time, there was a man who had been raised alongside dogs. Spaniels, terriers, Pekingese, Labradors. The man fell in love with a woman who had grown up in a small apartment with no pets at all. They married. Had a daughter who wanted a cat or maybe a dog. They told her having a brother would be like a pet but better. Had a son. The brother was harder to pick up than a puppy or kitten and significantly less furry. And the man missed dogs.

One day he came home with a black-and-white puppy in a cardboard box. The puppy did puppy things: chewed shoelaces, slept, tried to escape the house, succeeded in escaping, was captured. She was potty-trained, learned to sit and to heel. All that.

The puppy became a dog. But still lolloped. Still liked to leap and bound. Still exposed the pink strip of stomach to anyone who would have her.

Then the man started to think. One of the things he thought and said was that women who don't have babies can go – *a bit strange.* He said this to his daughter and made a wavy gesture with his hand to indicate the strange things that might happen to a woman without a baby.

The daughter was in the thick of her teenage years. Her body was stretching and changing out of her control. Still, she didn't think a baby would make her any less strange.

The woman said she already had one dog and didn't want more.

What happened next? In the woman's words, he took the dog *to be raped*. He didn't tell the woman in advance. He didn't tell the daughter. But he took his son. The two of them went to a farm.

The dogs were shut in a room together. At the end, their dog was pregnant. She became slow. Her belly hung down and her nipples, which were once hidden under a skim of fur, bulged.

Time skittered on. The boy was soon to be thirteen. He asked for a puppy for his birthday. The parents said *maybe* in the sort of voice that sounded like *yes*. A boy should have his own dog, the father believed. The daughter's feelings weren't hurt. She liked to wander the house at night and lived half-buried in a computer, eating midnight apples. No one was asking her to take care of anything.

The dog's belly grew heavier. She seemed tired. Sometimes she dug listlessly in the garden and the father said that was because she knew she was pregnant. An instinct. Proof the dog knew what she was doing.

All the family went out to lunch for the boy's birthday. It was a frigid February, the weather that day hovering just above freezing. They wrapped themselves into coats and jackets and scarves. They left the house warm for the dog who was dozing. Outside the house was a lightwell and the lightwell door had a dog flap to allow the dog to relieve herself when need be. Pregnant dogs need to urinate more often.

The family came back from the meal, warm and jolly. In the lightwell was a dark shape. A puppy. Dead by the time they rushed to it. Two others lay abandoned inside. The dog was whining, quivering, her tail low and tucked. She waddled towards her people. She had to be encouraged to lie down. She was still giving birth.

Animals, like people, do not always know what they are doing. The family speculated that perhaps she thought that giving birth inside was forbidden. They hushed her and soothed her and still she was giving birth to puppies barely larger than mice. Their eyes squeezed shut.

She ran her tongue over their backs. *She's cleaning them,* the father and mother said. Then she swallowed two. There were puppies and then there weren't. The parents said maybe there was something wrong with those puppies. She bit another puppy in half.

Let me break out of this third person now. I am not giving you gore for gore's sake. But I need you to flinch. I need you to understand that I had watched video after video about the dangers of pregnancy in school. But I had never seen this hot sticky mess. Had never seen the amber fear in the dog's eyes. Later, I'd read a Roald Dahl story where a rabbit did something similar. At the time, I was not prepared.

Back to the story:

After the freezing, the leaving, the eating – there were five left. Three black-and-white and two brown-and-white. Four strong healthy bodies and one small one. Four that the dog let suckle from her teat and the last she nudged away.

The girl knew at once the one she wanted them to keep. The smallest. A boy. *Adrian, like Adrian Mole because he looks like a mole.* But the dog would not feed Adrian. They were afraid she would eat him too, if pushed. The mother called the vet. The vet said that they were to feed the puppy water from a pipette. If Adrian survived the night, then he could have formula in the morning.

The mother rooted around in the medicine cupboard and found a pipette from some childhood medicine. Ears? Eyes? The need was forgotten. But it would do.

Can we keep him? the daughter asked.

We'll see, said the father.

The girl loved the puppy. His body was barely longer than the palm of her hand. The vet said that the puppy would need to be given water every three hours. The girl said she would stay up. The girl had insomnia. She was prepared for this moment. She lay on the floor next to him. The vinyl was cool against her cheek. She stroked his smooth back. The hair of new puppies lies completely flat. He couldn't fasten his mouth around the pipette but she dripped in the water. She lay close to him hoping her body would keep him warm. Hoping that he wouldn't know that his mother had pushed him away. She told him his name was *Adrian.* She told him she loved him. It would be one of two times in her life that she felt love at first sight.

Eventually his mouth stopped opening. His paws ceased to move. The vet said there was probably something wrong with his heart. The girl could never have saved him.

The girl had tried to kill herself. The details you don't need. When they touched her shoulder and said *There's nothing you could have done* – it seemed more indictment than comfort. An emphasis on both her and Adrian's failure. She thought about the few blurred bright moments that the dog had in its life. She wondered if Adrian had known something was wrong with him? Something unfit for survival?

The brother and the father picked a different puppy to keep.

What does it mean that the puppy died? Nothing? Everything? There is a special word for runt. But no equivalent for the biggest and strongest. Runts are the literal underdogs. The ones we want to root for. The ones who survive against all odds – well, apart from when they don't. The ones who should never have existed.

After giving birth, the family dog was never the same. She was slow and dozy. She hid from the puppy that the family kept. The puppy wanted to play by leaping on her back. In return she stole its food so often that the two dogs had to be fed separately.

For a long time, when I thought about not wanting children, I was thinking about the family dog.

I was thinking about the way she seemed to age completely. How she became cowed and sad. How she ran from her own child. Though dogs do not have episodic memories, I wondered if she remembered eating her own children. I thought, too, about Adrian. About what it means not to be strong enough to live. And how it feels to fail to save something you loved.

In 2019, I decided to get a dog. I had a home in which I felt safe. A partner who I trusted. Friends. More than one friend. I believed I could care for an animal. We asked around and were put in touch with a woman whose dog had had puppies.

We took the train to Lowestoft in Norfolk. When we got off, gulls cut through the air. I wondered if the puppies could smell the sea. We walked from the station. We were dressed formally, a little modestly, as if attending a human christening. My partner was wearing a button-down shirt, but the day was hot and sweat dotted his forehead. This was a meet-and-greet. We'd look at the puppies, to be sure they came from a safe, healthy home, not a puppy farm. The puppies' owners would quiz us about our ability to raise a dog. We wanted to impress them.

The retired couple admitted us to their bungalow. The sound of barking filled the hall.

They like to sing, the female owner said.

We sat in her sitting room and were introduced to the puppies. Their snouts had barely developed. They were all eyes and fluff. One of them stood out. She was smaller than a shoe. While the other puppies played with each other, she shuffled up and chewed my partner's lace. She was even tinier than the others and seemed to avoid them.

It wasn't her smallness that appealed. There are more miniature breeds. Chihuahuas, Japanese chins, Italian greyhounds are all more petite. It was the relative smallness, the fact that she seemed so left out – the runt.

Has anyone claimed her? we asked.

Not yet. Then the owner paused and mentioned that one person had dibs to choose a puppy before us. On the train home, I squeezed my partner's hand and said, *I love her. I love her so much.*

He reminded me that even if she was chosen by this dibs-person that she would have a good home. A safe home.

For the next few weeks, I woke up again and again in the night thinking of her. *What if she does come to us and we can't care for her?*

My mother would love her, my partner flung his arm around me. And, *Don't worry, you will.*

We bought a yarn dinosaur, a soft bed, a safe play pen. I told myself that we could do it. I read books. Watched videos.

We learned she could be ours. They told us we'd have to sign a contract, that we'd feed her and walk her and not leave her in a crate too long. That we would never sell her on or attempt to breed from her.

She came home close to the bottom of her breed's weight range. A few weeks later, she became ill. Throwing up yellow bile. We made her rice with white meat chicken. She sniffed it and refused. Her little face twisted away from the food.

What's wrong? I asked the vet. He told me to hold off feeding her until she was hungry. But she only got sicker. Thin yellow vomit. He told me her stomach lining was absorbing itself due to lack of food. Still, she wouldn't eat.

He prescribed a low dose of the medication they give chemotherapy patients to reduce their nausea. She ate.

Then it happened again. And again. The same pattern. She grew slowly, slowly. We tried different brands of dog food. She began to hold it down.

Though always she sniffs the food first, suspicion in her twitching nose.

Today she weighs just under five kilos, at the low but not bottom end for her breed. Somehow, she persuaded us to let her sleep on the bed. She tries to fight London's foxes standing on her back paws to appear larger. She is scared of the vacuum cleaner and the very fierce dog she sees reflected back at her from every window. Sometimes, she still unaccountably refuses to eat. But she survives.

I don't know how close the scales of fate were to tipping away from survival. What makes one runt safe and another slip away?

I don't believe women or bitches go mad when they don't breed. I don't know whether we'll have a child. Our dog was not practice for such an act.

How could she be? I will protect her for her whole life. I will feed and talk to and love her from the safety of our home and easy walks. A child is something else. A child must learn to live in the wilderness alone. It must be strong in other ways. It will face larger dangers.

I think of Adrian sometimes. I remember what it felt like to watch a small heart stop beating.

But if we do, I hope I have enough to help it survive.

Daphne

Esmé Weijun Wang

1.

A psychic from Brisbane told me I'd learn much from my dog about how to live. It was 2014. Daphne, the family dog, had been with us for two years. I was intrigued by the notion – at the time, my husband and I were already head over heels for our little mutt – but had no concept of what wisdom she might impart. As far as I could tell, she was a typical dog, with typical doggy desires. Daphne loved to catch a ball; she was fond of belly rubs. She was thrilled to doze in a sunbeam. If anything, I thought, she might teach me how to be present in a busy life that felt full of looking at the next task. But that was it.

2.

2014 was the same year that I was diagnosed with complex post-traumatic stress disorder, which to this day expresses itself most nightmarishly in its flares. Such flares include an excruciating sensitivity to the world that suddenly seems too loud and bright; any movement in my surrounds, including the slightest nearby shift, causes a startle or flinch. If I were in persistent danger, such symptoms could be life-saving. As they were, being in high alert without respite wore at my body and mind. I never knew how any day would go. I spent the hours feeling as though I were running on a treadmill that was going much too quickly, regularly going to bed at five in the afternoon because it felt too exhausting to stay awake any longer.

3.

What my husband and I know about Daphne's beginnings are sketchy. She was originally a stray from Shafter, a small town in southern California with an agricultural bent, and placed in a high-kill shelter before Rocket Dog Rescue in San Francisco brought her north for a hopeful adoption. They had no idea what breeds lay in her bloodline, though they thought she might grow to be approximately twenty pounds (ten years later, it's more like thirteen). They guessed at her age based on the status of her teeth and a certain kind of mite that she had, which were only present in young dogs. We adopted her at an event the rescue organisation held in a mall parking lot. She quietly rested in my lap on the drive home, and adapted easily to us over the first few months.

But I learned quickly that Daphne had certain peculiar behaviours among catching balls and asking for belly rubs. She had dramatic separation anxiety, once dashing pell-mell out of my parents' backyard door, which had been accidentally left ajar, to try and find us; I felt horrid for leaving her, knowing that she did not understand that we would, in fact, come back. And she avoided socialising with other dogs, and was downright aggressive when we once pet-sat for another dog.

And I was attempting to deal with my own traumatic responses. If C's movements and minor noises made for a particularly bad night, I'd go sleep alone in the guest room, which has a small twin bed and doubles as my office. Though saying so made me feel like I was also kicking feminism in the teeth, I told my therapist that I felt like a bad wife for doing it – sure, it wasn't my *fault*, but it meant that any kind of night-time intimacy was usually out of the question. I'd flee the bedroom more nights than not, leaving Daphne and C to their slumber.

4.

But I wasn't alone.

Daphne's peculiar behaviours included the following: if we were cuddling and I moved even slightly, she'd jump up and move across the room. No amount of coaxing could bring her back.

When Daphne first left me after a gesture or fidget caused her to go away, I was hurt as though a scorned lover. I'm embarrassed to admit that I usually got up, picked her up and brought her back to me as she squirmed, thereby bucking her instinct for my own desires. It wasn't even that I just wanted to snuggle, though that was certainly part of it. I didn't want to feel like I'd harmed her or scared her. I didn't want to feel abandoned by her because of something small and thoughtless. I wanted us to act like I hadn't done anything to make her go away.

5.

I began to put the pieces together of the events that had caused my complex PTSD. I called my mother, who lives in Taiwan, and told her what I thought had happened; I asked her why she'd done what she'd done. (Let there be no misunderstanding: she did not abuse me.)

'I thought that as long as you had clothes and a roof over your head and food to eat, that I was doing a good job,' she said. She was barely into her twenties when I'd been born in the Midwest, and psychologically fragile, herself.

At night I screamed and hyperventilated myself awake again and again. Daphne would jump onto the bed and frantically lick my face until I could finally feel calm enough to try and sleep once more. I loved her more with every year.

It took me a while, but finally, after she had jumped away from my body for the umpteenth time due to startle, I let her be. I began to draw her instead, sketching her wispy tail and narrow, pale snout with ink. In this way, I could be with her without being with her.

It took me a while, but I forgave myself for sleeping in the office.

The Rule of Paw

Sharlene Teo

The footsteps start every morning, around six. Sometimes late at night. Thud, thud thud. Bang bang bang. I live alone in a soulless new-build in west London. For the past six months I thought I was being terrorised by a child upstairs with a heavy tread. I pictured some deviant kid with a jam-streaked face and a frantic desire to run everywhere. The giant baby from *Spirited Away* fucking thumping, galumphing in its nappies.

Happy tantrums. Maybe it was a spooky ghost, an ex-morning person, and no one lived up there.

Last week someone in my building told me that the couple upstairs have a huge dog. I've since seen the culprit of my shortened sleep around. He's a hypoallergenic red-brown bundle of energy. I hear every tap of his tail against the wooden floors we all share. Labradoodle is happy, so so happy. He runs and wags. I usually love dogs. I've made it a personality trait. I used to wave around my old phone case festooned with different dog breeds. I frequently get dog-related gifts from my friends. I am a friend to all dogs. But not this one. I won't say I hate him, but I'm not a fan. Half-awake, I hear him scampering. He never barks. But he makes his weight known. My next-door neighbours hear him as well.

What can I do about it? Nothing.

I think about the dog I've wanted for at least half a decade. Every year that I put off getting one, I'm delaying the ageing of this phantom dog. I can stall that, though not my own ageing. The rule of paw states (anecdotally?) that for every human year, a dog ages sevenfold. I grew up with dogs, back home in Singapore: two border collies – a father and a son. Lancelot and Gawain. Lance passed away in 2008, Gawain in 2012. Sometimes I dream about them. They often talk. Their voices are wise, unaccented and urbane. They say things like: *Hello Shar! I love you. It's been a while. Everything will be OK. Don't worry. Everything will be OK.* Sometimes I wake up with tears on my face. I wasn't even the best dog owner. I'd sit with them, cuddle them, walk them, then go away. I was preoccupied with the fractional sum of early life, teenager things. Singapore is so humid. In their varicoloured fur coats, Lance and Gawain must have been so hot and uncomfortable. Border collies of farmland and field, stuck in a small garden and middle-class patio in Bukit Timah. When I snuck home from gross clubs late at night Lance would walk me from the gate to the door – not a long way, but just to make sure I was safe. Gawain would put his nose under my wrist when I was watching television. He loved attention. We watched many things together this way. Sated by affection, he liked to wriggle on the cool marble floor. I have never met anyone more delightful than Gawain.

After a family dog passes away, I don't think one ever fully stops missing the unconditional, ambient love of a sentimental companion. It's bound up so intimately with the mourning of childhood, the pernickety, annoying, comforting always-being-together of a household. I can't think of the last time my family of five were in the same room – not even fighting, just present. 2014? 2017? Christmas perhaps. Barbed air. The clench of a jaw. The death of our family dogs. Ergo the death of a storybook concept of family. An ungathering. That loss the petless cannot comprehend, might even find trivial. It's not frivolous. I'll miss these dogs until I die. They were always there. And then really conspicuously not. Lance and Gawain embedded in the rhythms and fabric of our family routine. The way we lost them inevitably. To time, to age. Old dogs forgoing energy. Puppy to grump. But still. The thump of a wagging tail. The vitality of that. The hopefulness. The trust and ease of wearing your heart on your sleeve. How happy they were just to go for a walk in the wrong climate.

I kept a pet chicken and a pet quail for a period. Lance herded them in the garden. He'd keep his muzzle low to the ground, moving with a watchfulness that was more paternalistic than predatory. My chicken and quail would hurry along in the grass, the chicken extending its wings and occasionally breaking into half-flight. Lance was king of the kitchen floor, king of our small garden. He was scared of nothing but rain. When it stormed heavily, he'd creep up to the bedroom I shared with my sister, shivering and whining very softly. Oh, I loved him. We always said he looked like Richard Gere. Something about the princely arrangement of hair and face. The dignified way he ate and shat, casting a look: *Do you mind?*

When he was a young dog, Lance followed my father to Myanmar when he was posted there for two years. They had a long, lush garden, bookended by a jetty. The sea glass of Inya Lake. Lance jumped in once or twice. My father and I used to exchange faxes. I don't recall how the ritual started, nor who suggested it. My father would always write to me, without fail. This was sometime before emails. I remember standing beside the beige fax machine, waiting for each missive to grumble and unfurl itself into being, how thin fax paper was the consistency of receipts. My father wrote to me about his office day, about Lance in the garden. I would complain about schoolwork. The handwritten effort of our actions. I wish the ink on those faxes didn't fade. My mother raised us and worked. She was always angry. Understandably, I now realise. We'd visit Yangon in summer. We watched VHS tapes and tried to eat silkworms. We visited pagodas. Five of us then, we rarely argued. When I think about that time now, mid-nineties, gauzy and inaccurate with the patina of touristic nostalgia, how happy Lance must have been. To have that garden, a field to run around in! Geckos to chase. Our dog a black and white blur amidst green and dirt-red.

It was my older brother's idea to matchmake Lance as Lance hit middle age. We found another border collie named Coco, sleek and stylish, a younger lady, so predictable! They really hit it off. They doggy-styled everywhere. Yuck! It was disturbing. From the litter we picked the fattest puppy. Gawain. Son liked to irritate father. But they loved each other. One summer, both dogs were infested with ticks. The insects, fat and red and wriggly, found their way all over the house. We lifted the skirt of one of my Barbie dolls and found a line of ticks resting on her thermo-plastic leg. Lance and Gawain wandered around depleted, blood-drained. The problem was solved with strong medicine.

Time wore on. Lance took longer and longer naps. He sighed a lot. He seemed tired of every-thing. Over It. When he passed away, Gawain was noticeably bereft. The forever-baby lost a bit of his impishness. It was painful to see. I had moved to

England by then for law school. Gawain looked lonely in the small patio. A gap on the tiles where his father used to lie beside him. Every time I came back, I'd cuddle Gawain and feel guilty about all the life I was living elsewhere. How the dog-shaped love in my heart was shrinking and fading due to distance and adult distractions. Presence into anecdote. Family into biographical data. Best friend into just another name.

When Gawain died suddenly, I remember getting a call from my parents as I was walking through Norwich city centre. I cried in some cafe, feeling sad and bad about loving Gawain so much but never enough. I'd flippantly wished he lived forever, so I could abandon him every year. That impulse nested a gauche, gooey complacency that was mawkishly worse than not caring. Pretending to care but not acting upon that care is perhaps crueller than unapologetically not caring. You can't have your cake and eat it. You can't have your dog and leave it. I think about all the news stories from animal shelters about lockdown puppy adoptions and people giving back the animals once real life or some semblance of it returns. You can't half-own a dog. A dog is not a machine. I avoid thinking about anyone's health because it threatens the stability of lapsed or dormant relationships with other bodies that get afflicted by time. We hate to face it. It's only human, it's only doglike. The rule of paw is fucking cruel. Lance lived for twelve years, eighty-four in dog years; Gawain around nine, sixty-three in dog years. He died young: *It was just age*, the vet said. Gawain was a runt, his balls never descended, he had an eternally puppyish quality. My brother and parents have sworn off ever getting another dog. They miss Lance and Gawain too much, they say. You can't fully replicate an era. There's a faithfulness to this kind of mourning, a fidelity to the irreplaceable trueness of who they were. Anthropomorphism? Sure.

Unlike the material world of real dogs with their real health problems, the internet offers an endless supply of puppies who seemingly never age. On TikTok or Instagram you can curate a feed of other people's companions doing cute/strange/noteworthy things. Dogs on the internet make heart eyes and do funny things and sweetly misbehave. A few years ago, when I was going through the worst period of my life, I stumbled across the ECAD puppy camera stream. ECAD stands for Educated Canines Assisting with Disabilities. The golden retriever puppies snuggle and nap, they climb on top of each other, they eat and play. It is almost too pure to witness the early days of a life that will be spent doing worthy and helpful things. I used to keep the tab open at all hours and check in every day. It was the cutest way to avoid my problems. Puppies punctuated the tortuous and flailing composition of my PhD thesis. Puppies soothed me and made my heart ache because I could not afford a dog; I was (and perhaps still am) too irresponsible and peripatetic.

Back in 2016, dog memes were burgeoning in popularity. My friends and I were members of a Facebook community called Cool Dog Group whose posts were charged with a feverish, competitive fervour for all things doggo, pupporino, etc. The idiolect was cloying but the pictures were good. I came to see dog memes as expressions of millennial angst: to own a dog was aspirational, it signalled you had settled into a neighbourhood, you knew its parks, you maybe had a partner to share the walking and fawning duties, perhaps a precursor to having children. Dogs, with their needy and people-pleasing natures, require a lot of attention. To be able to provide that indicates the owner can somewhat manage their time, at least for a walking and feeding routine. Dog owners get fresh air every day. Dogs demand a bigger lifestyle shift and more responsibility than the relative compactness and self-sufficiency of cats. Dogs can be a status symbol depending on type and breed. Trendy dogs like Shiba Inus and French bulldogs may indicate a predilection for chicness or internet irony. Rescue dogs can act as barking virtue signals. Tiny dogs suggest you don't mind yapping. Big dogs connote you have the space for them and the tolerance to pick up gigantic shits. The devotion a dog shows towards a piece of food is a constant reminder of the universal desire for satiation and instant pleasure.

To 'pet' someone is a sign of everyday affection. If it's a dog or cat, the attention is generally welcome. If it's a human, it really depends on the context; it can either feel consoling or condescending or terrible. As a pre-teen, I thought 'dogging' meant walking your dog. I thought 'heavy petting' meant owning a very large animal. My earlier naivete seems laughable, amusing. Yet now that so much time has passed since I owned dogs myself, it's as if I never had first-hand experience of living with them at all. Dogs remain an idealisation, so long ago since I knew any better of what it's like to love them up close, lose them unforgettably. I distrust people who don't like animals. Unless this stems from a childhood fear, I think there's something inherently shifty and hardened about a total detachment from the animal world. I assume dog owners are capable of casual tenderness and the necessary flexibility and compromise that arises from cohabitation. I like to think I too will be capable of this, someday. Shared space and bits of fur on the bed. Chewed-up shoes and a mess in the kitchen. The mantle and gratification of being a favourite person, the centre of the universe, unquestioningly loved.

Every year I tell people I'll finally get a dog if I get some massive book deal, conscious of the extraordinary and frankly unlikely conditions of this deferral. Yet work-adjacent or simply miscellaneous excuses pop up that keep me away from my house for long, erratic hours. I think of a phantom dog, lonely at home, resting its head on its paws. I think of a phantom dog getting old and disappointed by my absences and patchy affections, and it makes me wince. Visually I love Cavalier King Charles spaniels the most with their gumdrop faces and doleful eyes, their flappy little ears and mid-size. But they have all kinds of health problems and they don't live for very long. I want a dog that doesn't get lonely or ever die. I would call my dog Macaroni. I've said that for a long time. I won't get a border collie ever again out of loyalty, I think; unless I start a family and own a large field. Big dogs demand space and time. Every night the big dog upstairs clambers and clobbers around on the wooden floor, reminding me of its presence. How eavesdropped but real it is, how heartbreaking, how cumbersome, this boundary between animal and human. On the canal path I coo at other people's dogs. Sometimes I ask for permission to pet them and as I do that, I imagine a warmer, fuller kind of life.

Because Rescues Go Both Ways

alice hiller

Sometimes, a small brown dog flickers at the corner of my vision. I only ever saw her twice. Both times I was sitting outside a cafe that catches the December sun in Almería. With the subtlety of shadow, this stray darted out of a backstreet. Using the edges of buildings for cover, she slipped round the square, then dipped in between the legs of the cafe tables, searching for scraps.

She was clearly a regular, tolerated by the owner. At the time, Spain was overwhelmed by recession. About the size of a terrier, this dog was either an abandoned pet, or born from one. One ear looked injured, and her fur was scabbed in places. Her swollen teats showed she was a nursing mother, with puppies hidden nearby. Fighting to keep them and herself alive, she was lightning-quick, purposeful and wary.

I was travelling with my own dogs at the time, two grey-and-white terriers who watched her closely. I had driven with them to southern Spain for a month, to put myself back together after ovarian cancer. Many days it rained. When the sun shone we balanced along harbour walls, climbed ruined Moorish castles, or followed sheep tracks into vertiginous mountain stillness, as winter softened into spring and my energy grew stronger.

Alongside reclaiming myself beyond the surgery and treatment, while living in Spain, I was also seeking words to hold my childhood experience of being groomed and then sexually abused by my mother. For six years prior to diagnosis, my abdominal symptoms had been repeatedly dismissed by my GP as somatisations of the sexual abuse. Complications following the initial operation were similarly disregarded by consultants for two years, before finally being investigated and resolved through further surgery. Having come through so much, I hoped to give creative witness to what had been done to me as a child. I also wanted to help transform awareness around this crime, and open more pathways towards understanding for those of us living in its aftermath.

Whether in Spain, or back home, finding a way to write about those times was nonetheless intensely difficult. Hesitant about personal exposure, initially I framed my experiences with the distance of a novel. By trial and error, I came to understand that I needed to articulate what had happened to me more directly, and in my own voice. Through this process, as during my cancer treatment, the whiskered, frisky presences of my terriers, Toby and Feldspar, sustained me. They greeted each morning as another brilliant adventure, and guarded me with steady loyalty as I wrote.

When I eventually lost them, fourteen months apart, to old age, part of who I was seemed to go with them. I felt unanchored in the world. For two years, the project of writing around my childhood became the focus. Eventually it took shape as a collection of poems which I titled *bird of winter*, to encompass also living beyond the abuse. Working on this, I travelled to Paris and Brussels, and other places I had lived growing up. Back in London, I walked the same walks I had taken with Toby and Feldspar. Only dog-less. And then, as *bird of winter* neared completion, I realised the sorrow was somehow shifting. Tracking my former paths of mourning was now readying me to welcome a new dog into my life.

I knew I wanted to offer a home to a foreign rescue dog. This was to honour the memory of the courageous Spanish stray, and other dogs like her I had seen on my travels, and because shelters abroad face greater demands, with fewer resources. Once I began looking, in the summer of 2019, scrolling through rows of alert faces, from sweet puppies to the massive, hopeful, descendants of shaggy working dogs, my longing became acute. One tense evening, my husband identified five wonderful but entirely unsuitable dogs he wanted us to adopt. In reality, our future companion needed to be suited to living in London, and also travelling to near Oxford, where I curate a small sculpture museum and archive. Not all rescues thrive in cities, or meeting strangers.

Fortunately, we agreed on a young dog on the Wild at Heart site who seemed the right fit. She was seven months old, in Vasilia's shelter on the Greek island of Lesvos. An intuitive woman, with a profound empathy for animals, Vasilia works miracles with minimal resources, mainly by her skilful management of her canine charges. Like so many people running shelters, she has built hers up over twelve years, a little at a time. Help has come from friends, when they can give it, and donations from the local community, and now support from the charity.

After further careful discussion, my husband and I applied for our hoped-for dog, then I set off alone to Dieppe for four days of researching and writing. Alongside witnessing the sexual abuse to which I was subjected as a child by my English mother, the poems in *bird of winter* also honour the good I experienced, which helped me reclaim life. For this reason, I wanted to revisit the area in Normandy where I had stayed every summer with my French grandmother or *bonne maman*. Being loved by her had helped me know my worth as a human being, irrespective of my mother's cruelty and predation. I needed to draw on that energy as a force for healing within the collection.

The studio I rented was four floors above Dieppe's inner harbour. Like fishes sliding between each other in deep water, boats of all sizes come and go day and night. Walking along the seafront in the evening, the Phare d'Ailly still striped the sky with fingers of light, as it had when I saw them from my bedroom window in my grandmother's house. By day, I returned to beaches I played on with her and my father. Alone, under the changing autumn skies, watching the clouds reflected in the sand flats, it felt as if time was holding me, letting closed doors open.

Then, on a day of sheeting rain, and pavements running with water, I got the call that we had passed the assessment. The dog we had tentatively named Ithaca would be coming to join us later that month. I was watching a fishing trawler manoeuvre into a mooring, the sailors working on the shining deck in yellow waterproofs. I wanted to hug someone and shout for joy. In a break in the weather I ventured out along the seafront. Grey waves surged against the concrete harbour wall. New strength was entering my life when I needed it most. Finishing *bird of winter*, whose wings opened out of the saddest and most desperate times, I would once again have the closeness of a loyal companion snoozing at my feet, or chivvying me out into the breathing, changing world.

Once I knew Ithaca would soon be with us, I could allow myself to dwell on the photos we were sent. Golden brown, with a white chest and paws, and the most beautiful hazel eyes, she was found aged three months with her sister and mum. A known street dog, Ithaca's mother had managed to care for her puppies in an abandoned building, like the stray in Almería. Just two years old herself, their mother was the first to be adopted. Once Ithaca and her sister were in good condition, they were ready to join a cohort of dogs travelling to the UK in October, whom I would be meeting.

A Wild at Heart video gave us an idea of the world Ithaca was leaving. It opens to dry earth, and gold late-summer grass, under olive trees. A series of wire-fenced pens and shelters, with green tarpaulins stretched out for shade, are spaced between the trunks. The camera cuts to dogs rushing to the mesh walls to greet Vasilia. She reveals that the different enclosures were built, one at a time, as funds could be gathered together, by her and her friends and supporters.

We learn Vasilia comes every day to feed her dogs, clean out their pens and offer playtime.

The video shows them running to and fro in the central area, bouncing up, twining themselves around her. She explains that this is the 'lobby' where she socialises the dogs and gives them treats, group by group, before they go back into their pens for food. This nurture helps former strays and street dogs, who may have been maltreated by people, rebuild their confidence. If animals of all kinds have been either abandoned, or violently chased away, or otherwise subjected to harm, that fear needs to be unlearned before rehoming can be viable. Reflecting their different circumstances, some dogs on the Wild at Heart site are identified as needing to be the only dog in a home, or to live in a quiet or rural environment. Others are not suitable for mixing with children.

Wild at Heart told us that Vasilia's dogs are among the best at adapting to their new lives, probably because of her sensitivity to their needs, and ability to assess the dogs she takes in and place them together in groups where none feel threatened. She has also found a few families able and willing to foster on Lesvos, which can help acclimatisation. Because she knows her dogs closely, she is also able to predict where they are likely to thrive, which can make a huge difference for dogs with troubled histories.

In the video Vasilia also introduces a pen of clearly elderly dogs. Some have been with her for up to ten years, without being adopted, often due to behavioural difficulties. Instead, she explains, 'they are growing old with me.' Such dogs need to be sponsored long term. When we were accepted to adopt Ithaca, we decided also to support another dog who needed lifetime shelter care – in recognition of Vasilia's work.

As part of the application process, we received a short video of Ithaca in the courtyard of a foster home where she was moved to prepare her for life in England. We also got extra photos, along with detailed guidance on welcoming a rescue dog into your family. Once I knew Ithaca was joining us, I went through everything many times, trying to imagine her character, and counting down to our meeting.

When the day finally came, Messenger updates tracked our dogs flying from Lesvos, to Athens, and then Brussels, before the final stage of driving by van through the Channel Tunnel. Many Europe-based charities drive their dogs all the way overland in specialised transports. A photo showed Ithaca peering out of the crate which she was sharing with Tilly. Both dogs had their noses through the wire. They looked keen to get out. Ithaca had half-climbed on top of Tilly to see better. Then they were in sunlight, on iridescent astroturf, getting fresh air while their paperwork was cleared for the Channel Tunnel. Low to the ground, tails tucked in, both sisters were being stroked for reassurance by the transport crew.

While Tilly's family was waiting in Norfolk, I was due to meet Ithaca at the second stop at Cobham Services, on the M25. By then our dogs had been travelling for more than twelve hours. It was dark when I got there around 6.30 p.m., with my mother-in-law as backup. Once the dogs arrived, we hurried to the coach park where the silver van was waiting, with its door already slid open.

Ithaca had been lifted out of her crate and was placed in my arms. In the blur of receiving her, I took in that the other dogs were relaxed and calm. Tilly would be travelling on with her shelter mates to Norfolk. Holding Ithaca's young, warm body close to me, I stepped down from the van. In the murky half-light, with the distant roar of cars on the M25, I sensed her trembling. Breathing in the biscuity smell of her soft fur, I whispered that I was her person. I was claiming her, one animal-self to another. I had not been able to help that small brown stray in Spain, but now my chance had come. I would give Ithaca everything I could.

Once I'd stepped out of the van, I put Ithaca down, for a few brief moments, on the grass verge, in case she needed to wee. I saw immediately that she was too scared, however. Carrying her to my car, I settled her in the back with my mother-in-law for reassurance. The photo I took shows Ithaca looking bewildered, sitting straight up. Forty minutes later, we were home. Her first proper meal all day was waiting. Chicken and rice, as instructed. Ithaca ate it in moments – and then began to settle, exploring the pile of toys. Already, a different dog was emerging. The next photo that evening she is sitting on our sofa, a chew clamped between her paws, beginning to feel safe.

As a dog who spent her first three months hidden wherever her mother could find a safe resting place on the streets, for Ithaca darkness was clearly a time of great risk. Drunks might be stumbling around, or packs of boys looking for dogs to chase and scare. The car lights, noises and shadows of the car park probably brought back that fearfulness. Being fed and shown warmth and affection in a lighted, secure home signalled that Ithaca had arrived somewhere where she would not be hurt.

Ithaca ventured with me into our small back garden, but she was too intimidated to pee outside that first dark night, using an absorbent pad indoors. From the following morning onwards, however, she proved 'house-trained', probably because she had stayed briefly with a foster family before coming to the UK. Not all rescue dogs are initially. Intently watching a dog peeing in the park, and then others going to the toilet when we were out and about, Ithaca realised that these were additional alternatives to using the garden – and followed their examples.

Ithaca had lived on the streets, in a shelter and then a foster home, but inner-city life was unknown. As she must have in Lesvos, she was constantly observing dogs around her and teaching herself what she understood were the rules. Each time she noticed something different, she would look at me, for confirmation, and then when I told her yes, incorporate this into her routine. This also applied to allowing people to greet or stroke her, and welcoming new people who came to the house, and later exploring off-lead in the park.

Bed on that first night was also a time of discovery. Once we were ready, I carried Ithaca up the tight cast-iron spiral stairs to my bedroom, where

Toby and Feldspar previously slept. We settled down with me underneath the duvet, Ithaca on top, lying alongside my leg. She was grounding and anchoring herself. While we rested together, there was love already in our closeness. The following morning, her eyes opened as mine did. The delight on her face said *'You're still here!'* With my encouragement, she commando-crawled up for a cuddle.

From those first moments, Ithaca formed an intense bond with me. I never had to wonder where she was – because wherever I was, she was there too. As part of her determination for us not to be separated, she instantly taught herself how to snake her body round the tight corkscrew of the spiral staircase on her second day, after I went down momentarily without her. While they each learned to scamper nervously up, Toby and Feldspar always had to be carried down, scared by the drop visible through the cast-iron treads. Fortunately, I work mainly from home, and if I needed to go further afield, I could leave Ithaca with my mother-in-law as a trusted sitter, until she became secure enough to be left alone.

Ithaca also formed a warm connection with my husband when he came to meet her on Friday night, two days after she arrived. Because he only saw her on weekends, it took until the end-of-year holidays, once they were able to spend extended time cuddling up together, for them to become inseparable. The fact that my husband eats meat, and I do not, further cemented their bond. Now, every Friday, Ithaca greets him ecstatically, yelping with delight. She leaps up to lay her head against his leg, while hugging his knee with her front paws. He calls this his 'hero's welcome'. It lasts five minutes and is the highlight of his week. Conversely, when the time to say goodbye comes on Sunday evening, Ithaca's tail is down, and they are both equally dejected.

Fortunately, Ithaca is also completely devoted to my two adult sons, and loving towards my closest friends, whose names she recognises when I say they are coming, along with her beloved dog-sitter and her two daughters. Wild at Heart advises a gradual introduction to everything, and these people came into her life one at a time as her confidence developed. Like many rescues, Ithaca was tentative about the outside world. She investigated the garden bush by bush, and gathered the toys I collected for her into careful piles, to which she added sticks from our walks, together with 'found' treasures including oven gloves and a dustpan and brush.

Reflecting her gradual increase in confidence, at first Ithaca kept her tail in a scared tuck between her back legs. After a few days, it rose into the feathered, upright curl that floats aloft as she walks. A week in, she proudly used her deep, beautiful bark to inform the foxes that the garden was *her* space. To begin with, parks and pedestrian crossings worried her. She kept herself pressed against my legs. These soon became safe. Even now, though, she avoids big groups of dogs or people. During her first weeks with us, Ithaca occasionally showed fear-aggression – growling or snarling if she felt we might take food or toys from her. This soon resolved. She was also amazed by the hugeness of police horses, freezing to stare at them, then standing with her paws against my knees, looking intently at my face to check what I thought.

Wild at Heart advises that no matter how young an abandoned dog may have been when brought to a shelter, having lived on the streets, they will have potentially been exposed to trauma. This can leave them less well equipped to cope with certain stresses without gradual habituation and support. Because my own childhood home was completely unsafe, as a result of the sexual abuse from my mother, I could relate to Ithaca's sense of fearfulness. I knew that she needed to be absolutely certain of my love, as I was of my French grandmother's. Whenever I visited *bonne maman*, outings were planned for us, my favourite foods waiting, with a pile of books to share. Ithaca's and my long twice-daily walks, with regular meals and fun play at home, gave the same reassuring message.

Perhaps because of having lived precariously at the start of her life, Ithaca also reads people acutely. When my elder son was struggling with jet lag and insomnia, Ithaca would open his bedroom door with her shoulder, and jump up to lie beside him. From her arrival, Ithaca was also aware of when life is more difficult for me, as a result of anniversaries relating to the childhood sexual abuse to which I was subjected. At these times, she becomes my watchful shadow, keeping close, nudging me with her nose to offer a cuddle or a play – trying to stop those cruel ghosts from rising and walking again.

While I was settling Ithaca into our family, I was also finalising my manuscript of poems. Early in January of 2020, on a radiantly sunny day, I took a train to Liverpool to meet the poet and editor, Deryn Rees-Jones. She told me that Pavilion Poetry, who are part of Liverpool University Press, would like to publish *bird of winter* the following year.

I had dreamed of this happening – but what came next was far from easy for any of us. As Covid-19 spread, first in China, then around the world, I was simultaneously opening myself to the darkness of my early life to write the final poems, and edit sequences together.

This meant repeatedly entering the emotional experiences of my child and teenage selves, at their most vulnerable, and allowing old, destructive energies to move within my waking and sleeping hours. Like many people, as the pandemic worsened, I was also trying to limit my social encounters. Living alone through the week, having Ithaca to walk and care for, became invaluable. She gave me continuous contact with loving energy – the opposite of what I knew as a child – and with it the courage to keep working on *bird of winter*.

When the lockdown came on 20 March 2020, Ithaca and I stayed in London, separately from my husband. He remained at home in Oxford, to avoid both of us getting ill, should his mother, who lives near him, need help. For the next eleven weeks, Ithaca was the only living being indoors with me, even as the walls of my mind seemed to be buckling and melting. During my childhood, my mother had threatened me with death to facilitate the abuse. Now it was visibly entering London's streets, turning the nights of that blossom-filled spring blue with the lights of ambulances.

Over and above the global casualties, most days of the week I was hearing of people close to people I knew dying. A friend in the next street lost two friends in the first weeks. My neighbour was unconscious in intensive care for three months. In Liverpool, Deryn Rees-Jones fell ill, and took many months even to begin to recover. As I heard these waves of news, I was still having to enter and re-enter the darkness of my childhood working on *bird of winter*. Through it all, Ithaca was my place of safety, and my rescuer.

With her golden-brown self, her hazel eyes, her mobile, long-nosed face, frowning and puzzled in one moment, joyous in the next, she called me back to life. On our walks, her white paws kept pace with me. She stood beside me as I heard of another person taken to hospital, another elderly parent lost to Covid-19, a private hospital quietly admitting old men to die because there was nowhere else to care for them. When Ithaca and I went out last thing at night, we witnessed the silent ambulances drawn up outside houses, or threading through backstreets, always together.

In the parks, Ithaca ran wide loops over the spring grass, sprinting past me with her ears flat to her head. She pranced up to, or sped past, other dogs, barking proposed games of chase. She found more sticks and food wrappers to carry home and add to her collections. When we walked along the river, she stood on her hind legs, with her front paws on the railings, peering down at the ducks and cormorants and moorhens, or trying to spot the pair of geese. The geese are her favourites because they occasionally fly up onto the riverwalk where she can examine them.

When we were reunited with my husband and mother-in-law, and my adult sons, Ithaca was rapturous with happiness. On weekends, she still resists going out for a walk without my husband.

If he is sleeping late, once home, Ithaca rushes upstairs to wake him and let him know that their separation has ended. In other ways, Ithaca's rescue heritage remains her identity. On the streets, she always recognises and greets fellow shelter dogs, who recognise her too.

It is as if the experience of living on the streets and in shelters switches on an additional part of their brains, and they register this unconsciously in each other. Comparably, over the years, I have found that my close friends often later reveal that they, like me, have had complex experiences growing up, or that these have taken place within their immediate family history. For dogs and humans alike, it is perhaps a matter of picking up an additional layer of receptivity. It may have been part of what led Ithaca and I to bond so strongly, and allows us still to find delight and reassurance every day in each other's company.

Curious, alert, always delighted to while away time in a cafe or make herself at home in a budget hotel room, Ithaca is also an ideal travel companion. Whenever we can, we head to Worthing for intense bursts of writing and extended beach explorations. On the shoreline, her body becomes curiosity on four legs. She dips her nose into tide pools, wades with me in the breaking waves, then races across the shining sand flats as if she were flying. Finding beach treasures, watching the waves rear and crest at high tide, or spotting fish from the end of the Victorian pier, all thrill her. When my thoughts go back to that small brown stray I glimpsed darting between cafe tables in Almería, I am so grateful that Ithaca's life turned out differently.

Tending

Jessica J. Lee

It is November, and I am seven months pregnant. As I write, my dog is curled next to me, melodramatically sniffing the pillow. Brisket wants my attention for the thousandth time today. I know this because every few minutes his voice quivers. He shuffles and sighs, offers a swift flick of the tail. I give in.

I did not set out to have such an attached, needy dog. I am not sure anyone does. I remember the lightness of going out for hours, not worrying about a creature I left at home. I remember when I didn't compulsively check the Dog Monitor app to see if he settled himself to sleep. When I didn't plan my days almost entirely around his creaturely need for companionship. I chose this attachment – just as I have chosen to have a child – but still, I am struck by how remarkably unpredictable dogs can be in how they upend our lives.

The months before Brisket came into our home, my husband and I painstakingly researched dogs. We had wanted one for years, but hadn't known our Berlin apartment allowed pets, until one afternoon I spotted another tenant leading their sheepdog through the courtyard. Immediately I secured permission to keep a dog from the landlord. We bought training books, researched local puppy schools. Discerned the process through which to acquire a municipal dog owners' licence and started a spreadsheet tracking our progress. We wrote to breeders across Germany and visited the local animal shelter. I began to feel a visceral longing for a puppy to nestle between us on the sofa. An ache where I wanted a dog. And I exercised my longing by planning.

I say this because it's important: I knew the kind of dog I was seeking. The temperament and tendencies. Trainability. We were mostly looking at shy but friendly and intelligent dogs – Kooikerhondjes, tollers and a rare German breed called the Kromfohrländer. I had some expectations of what our dog might be like.

And then, in late August 2019, I received a message from a Kromfohrländer breeder who'd had a litter of nine puppies, one of whom was much smaller than the rest. Eight of the puppies were spoken for, she told me, but she was searching for a family for the runt. He had a small cleft palate – *Gaumenspalte*, a new word for me in German – but his prognosis was good. He was the liveliest of his litter, despite his size and despite going hungry the first days of his life when he couldn't latch. She had eventually nursed him by bottle, and he learned to watch from a distance as his littermates suckled their mother. *Der kleine Kämpfer* – the little fighter – she called him. Would we be interested in giving him a good home?

Never in my research had I learned what a cleft palate would entail. I hadn't really known it to be a possibility in dogs – until recent years, most breeders and vets would simply have euthanised pups born with clefts. It wasn't exactly what we'd planned.

I forwarded the email to my husband at work. *What do you think?*

*

What determines the nature of a dog? Most guide-books will point to breeding: working-dog habits like heel-nipping are bred in, while the propensity to lounge in close proximity to humans is common to companion breeds. Despite vast differences in the breeds, all stem from one – or perhaps two – common ancestors.

15,000 years ago, give or take a few thousand, in Western Eurasia or East Asia or both, the act of domestication transformed the life of a wolf. That wolf's species is now extinct. But its descendants – in the form of grey wolves and domesticated dogs – remain.

Quite how the act of domestication took place remains unknown: whether a litter of wolf pups was captured and weaned by humans, or whether friendly wolves, seeking convenient access to food and warmth, ingratiated themselves among us. But the incremental changes recognisable in present-day dogs followed. A change in the ears, a recolouring of the coat, a tendency to dig or herd or cuddle. And these transformations, selectively bred by us, are vast: a recent dog genome study showed that genetic variation between breeds can be over 27 per cent (by comparison, human populations vary by roughly 5.4 per cent).[1]

But so too does a dog's environment reshape them: it is now fairly common practice that a well-bred dog should remain with its littermates and mother for ten weeks, learning much of the early socialisation needed to make it in Dog World. But what happens when a dog like Brisket spends those early weeks gaining all his sustenance from human hands?

Kromfohrländers are a very recent breed, in the grand scheme of dog history, with very little variation in their gene pool. Though most breeds we know emerged in the past few hundred years, Kromis came about only in the decade after the Second World War, during which Allied troops had taken to keeping strays as mascot dogs. After 1945, when many of them found themselves strayed again, one such dog – Original Peter, a Brittany griffon or terrier mix found along the French–German border – was taken in by a German woman named Ilse Schleifenbaum.

Ilse adored Peter, who was strong, intelligent, and showed himself to be a loyal companion. So Peter was set to breeding with a neighbour's fox terrier: first came a litter of gold-and-white puppies, and then six further litters when the first proved such pleasant companions. By 1955, the breed was recognised in Germany – named 'Kromfohrländer' in dialect for the crooked, furrowed land on which Ilse lived and bred her dogs.

Today, Kromis remain a rare sight in Germany, their numbers totalling around two thousand worldwide. Only a few hundred are born each year, with the breeding pool strictly controlled. Indeed, this small number has recently resulted in a breeding programme aimed at widening the gene pool by crossing Kromis with Danish–Swedish farmdogs, an effort that has proved divisive among breed purists.

Ideally – that is, *according to the breed characteristics* – Kromis should be rough or smooth-haired, with a piebald colouring in chestnut and white. They should be athletic in build, weighing 10–15 kg and measuring between 38–46 cm high. Their temperament tends towards shyness with strangers – both human and canine – and extreme loyalty to their owners. They aren't dogs I would describe as very social.

We learned quickly that Brisket has never been a textbook Kromi. His build is leaner than that of his siblings, owing perhaps to the slower start he had as a puppy. Before meeting him, I read through the chart recording his birth – its time and date, his weight, the order of birth. A few lines down, the breed association noted that his colouring was too pale, toffee hues barely registering against the stark white of his rough coat. He had no brown around his eyes, no blaze down the middle. The cleft in his soft palate and the small gap in his hard palate, too, were registered as flaws, the source of which is still unknown but produced most likely by a genetic cause.

Perplexingly, he is almost overly social – indeed, we've struggled to stop him from courting friendship with every stranger he sees. From his early days, his infatuation with newness, and with people, was apparent: he was the first to wander from his whelping box, the first to greet any visitor. When we visited him as a tiny pup, he climbed unbidden into my lap, though his siblings ignored us and huddled together. He was childlike – often unsure of himself around other dogs – and more prone to sit with us humans.

Of course, not all dogs exactly fit their breed description. But in the years I have had Brisket, I have wondered what makes a dog like him stray so wholly – and in this case, pleasantly – from expectations? Did early socialisation with humans cause this deviation from the norm? Like the first wolves to realise that human company meant care and sustenance, did hours spent suckling formula from a baby bottle teach him there could be a different order to this world?

*

Brisket came home to us when he was ten weeks old after a surgery repaired his soft palate, stitching the gap that opened towards his throat. Just a small fissure in his hard palate remained, but it was enough to keep us worried.

I joined Facebook groups for owners of cleft-palate puppies, learned all the ways in which their care differed from that of otherwise healthy dogs. I researched kibble, discerning which shapes and sizes could be swallowed whole and were least likely to get stuck in his cleft. I learned to withhold soft and pureed foods – too much of a risk for aspiration – and scoured our street for daily hazards: sticks that could wedge themselves in the roof of his mouth, shards of glass that could cut his pink, still-healing throat. I began his training not with 'sit', but with the commands 'leave it' and 'drop it'.

We spent our nights awake and worrying: he had a persistent sinus infection for the first month he was with us – likely from aspirating on puppy mousse before we knew better – and was plagued for months by ear infections. When his breath rattled, we got down on the floor next to his bed to watch his chest rise and fall. We worried we'd made a horrible mistake. That we weren't actually equipped to care for a dog whose needs were so specific, so different from other dogs we had known.

But he was, amidst the worry of those early weeks, more exuberant than I could comprehend. We took him to puppy classes, and his body pulsed with excitement at a room full of strangers. He didn't seem to know how to play with the other puppies – being either too shy or too brash – so spent most of the class quivering on my lap, learning how to stay calm in the presence of others. I carried him around Berlin in a sling, and his nose prickled at every new smell he encountered: doner kebab, crushed leaf, beer and woodsmoke. He climbed into the laps of friends and nuzzled up to elderly strangers on the tram. When friends brought their babies to say hello, he stood on his hind legs to gaze into their pushchairs. Every single thing seemed bright, held interest.

At home, at night, he lay cradled in my arms, head draped on my shoulder, as he had sat while nursing as a pup. Then he would tenderly clutch his favourite stuffed toy – a fuzzy llama we confusingly named Lamby – in his mouth, suckling a corner of its fabric as he dreamt. This, I read, was a habit common to puppies who missed out on nursing: a longing to recreate the intimacy they'd lost at the teat. Two and a half years on, he still falls asleep while suckling.

We'd been told Kromis tend not to overeat, so are good candidates for free-feeding. Brisket had – and still has – an inability to eat slowly, and an unwillingness to stop eating no matter how full he becomes. We portion out his food into slow-pour feeders, and cannot leave him loose where food bowls sit open and waiting. I've wondered if this habit is tied to a core memory, those early days when he couldn't latch and his weight rapidly halved. If his body remembers a time when no one yet knew he had a cleft. How he began life hungry, insatiable.

I will never know if Brisket could have been different. If he is the way he is because of his history. If he'd been born without a cleft, would he be more like his siblings? They're more typical of the breed, aloof and shy. They're inclined to distance from people, less fixated on nourishment and human affection. Whether it is a trick of genetics or a simple fact of socialisation, I cannot say for sure.

But I do know that his affection, his fixation on food, his tendency to suckle – all are common among cleft-palate dogs. These are dogs whose formative days are forged not with their own kind, but with tubes and bottles, with humans who stay up all night to feed them. When a cleft-palate pup resists feeding, the advice is to swaddle them. Like babies. The parallels are literal. Insistent.

I do not want to compare my dog to a baby. As I write, my actual human foetus presses a foot beneath my ribs, an elbow into my abdomen. They will be born in a few weeks' time.

The waiting for them is a different, stranger feeling than the longing I felt for a dog. But both, I know, demand a kind of care that borders on endless – on worry, watchfulness, and a kind of affection not specific to species boundaries. On that strange entanglement of genetics and early love that shapes us all. I cannot know how my affection will shape the person to come.

Behind me now, Brisket has curled his soft body into my enormous round pregnancy pillow. I tell my husband that once the baby is here, we'll need to keep the pillow. The dog loves it too much. And as I fill our house with sensory toys and books about developmental milestones, I think constantly about those early months with Brisket. When the world held only newness. When I couldn't really know the kind of dog he would grow into – but fell in love with the peculiar creature he was.

NOTE

1. https://www.americanscientist.org/article
   /genetics-and-the-shape-of-dogs

Fetch

Nell Stevens and Eley Williams

At puppy school, they taught us to communicate with our dog using hand signals rather than words. It was easier, we were told, for dogs to understand that an upturned hand with fingers scrunched together means *sit* than to understand that the word 'sit' means *sit*. During the classes, my wife Eley and I hovered over our puppy Bryher, and became practitioners of mime, or air traffic controllers, or semaphore flag wavers. Bryher regarded us stolidly, and with the air of someone tolerating a long, boring story from an elderly relative. She was always the last of the group to *sit*, or *lie down*, or *roll over*. At the end of the course, the puppy school teacher invited all the puppies except Bryher to come to puppy university. She said puppy university wasn't for everyone. I felt a passing impulse to put my hands over Bryher's (long, ridiculous) ears. 'Don't listen to her,' I muttered, which was unnecessary, since Bryher never listened to anyone.

At some later point, though, Bryher started to understand words. Eley and I talked to her constantly, and there was a day when I'd been walking with her in the woods near our house, throwing a ball for her and trying to persuade her to drop it so I could throw it again. One of my throws landed the ball in some undergrowth, and I poked around for it, narrating what I was doing to Bryher. 'Where's your ball?' I said, and then, just like that, as though she'd been waiting for me to ask, she went to where it was and nudged it into the open. The puppy who had taken weeks of cajoling to understand 'sit' now understood the question: 'Where's your ball?'

Communicating with Bryher remains a hit-and-miss endeavour. Sometimes she stands immobile, staring blankly, mouth cracked into a wide, panting smile, as we ask her, over and over, to go to bed. And she is not the kind of dog, much to my dismay, who will nuzzle your tear-stained face while you tell her about your bad day. But if you make a weird noise that she's never heard before, she'll come full force at you with joy, all wagging tail and lolling tongue as though she wants to taste the novelty, and if you throw her ball and follow it with the question, 'Where's your ball?' she will, fairly reliably——

——bring it back. Sharing space and knowledge can be its own game of fetch, or tug, or retrieval. Neither Nell nor I had grown up alongside dogs and so we committed to putting time aside for careful research, hoping to welcome Bryher in a state of informed readiness. This meant that before she had even hurtled over the threshold of our one-bedroom flat, new dog-related vocabulary became part of our lexicon: with best-intentioned paranoia, we learned from dry bullet-pointed textbooks how to spot *syringomyelia*; we bookmarked pages about the dangers of lapping pondwater if it showed signs of *harmful algal blooms*; various blogs that used expressions like *pupper, snoot* and *blep* waxed lyrical about the benefits of pushing bits of liver sausage into *KONG*™ and how to wrangle hindlegs into an *Equafleece*®. We took notes earnestly, testing the shapes and sounds of the new words and phrases with our mouths as if they were unfamiliar treats.

Theory only goes so far, and soon after Bryher scampered into our lives it became obvious that various awarenesses could only be learned on the trot. Knowledge was gleaned amongst the nettles of local parks or passed on to us by other dog walkers; we returned from walks and updated each other about emergent traits we observed, or potential issues regarding dogs, in general, and Bryher, in particular: *avoid that stretch of river path, there's a particular swan that's got it in for spaniels,* for example, or tips about how best to open poo bags at speed when wearing thick woollen gloves. It was our first year living together, so Nell and I were still in the process of understanding the patterns of each other and our new surroundings too. Just as shambling, delighted Bryher found a role as an intrepid guide around various wooded byways and stretches of green parkland that otherwise we would never have thought to explore, her presence also introduced new quirks, nuances and urgencies to our communication. The algorithms on our phones updated to accommodate our new panicked mode of googling, usually while hunched over a happily munching dog, so that any search requests beginning 'Is [noun]' now autocompleted with '__ toxic to dogs?'. At the same time, texts sent between Nell and me changed from the tender sweet nothings of our early relationship to far more briskly informative messages ('baking soda gets urine [dog] out of carpet'), or ones that resembled reconnaissance bulletins ('someone has dropped [??] whole Xmas pudding near junction and she is obsessed: avoid route if poss'), or were just monosyllabically exultant (a picture of Bryher staring up a besquirreled tree, captioned '*HELLLOOOO*').

The algorithms silently, assiduously adapted once again the following year when a baby joined our household. Whereas sharing care of a dog had involved a joyful but steep learning curve, and introduced new intricacies and useful bluntnesses to how we communicated with each other, the addition of a baby to this set-up meant further changes and adaptations; it did not escape our notice that——

——there is no puppy school for babies. The closest we got was a mid-pandemic NCT class over Zoom, during which people's heads bobbed in and out of view as they bounced on yoga balls and we were put in break-out rooms to discuss our anxieties about labour.

My main takeaway from the experience was that, while the other couples remained on screen as they watched the instructor hold up a plastic doll and a single knitted boob to her screen to demonstrate correct breastfeeding positioning, Eley and I were always getting up, coming back and then getting up again because we had to deal with the dog. She needed water, or she wanted to go outside, or she wanted to come back in again, or she had found an old book on a low shelf and was cavorting around the flat with it, leaving torn-up scraps of pages like confetti everywhere. 'We can't have a baby,' I said to Eley, once I'd noticed this. 'We don't have time. We already have a baby.'

Saying your dog is your baby felt like the sort of thing that would aggravate people who actually had babies. I knew this; I knew that when the real baby came I would no longer feel that Bryher was one. And once our son arrived, it was true that I was able to discern some subtle differences between the two of them. But there were also, undeniably, similarities: both were indescribably precious to us, both unbelievably demanding, and I desperately wished that both of them could speak.

My most vivid memories from the fuzzy early days of parenthood are of taking the baby out with the dog. It was often a disaster: Bryher, who mourned the loss of our full attention, would be boisterous and noisy, barking so loud she'd make the baby cry; or else I'd have the baby in the sling and have to perform a kind of sideways limbo to pick up poo without getting it anywhere near his face. People who watched this would often say something like, 'You've got your hands full,' and I wouldn't know how to respond because, yes, I literally did.

Eley and I learned quite quickly that the dog and the baby were easier to deal with separately. And so one of us would be on baby duty and one of us on dog duty, and it worked much better, except, I realised, we saw so much less of each other than before. It seemed the great paradox of parenthood was that it bound us together irrevocably, and yet we hardly ever got to hang out any more——

——and when we were able to snatch moments together, just the two of us, it felt necessary to exploit the sudden luxury of being inattentive while in company. We are on high alert a lot of the time now, sometimes without even realising: it takes just a second of looking the wrong way and Bryher has eaten a relative's hearing aids, to give one harrowing and expensive case in point; one lapse of concentration and our son has dropped a foam toy train on his foot and his world has dissolved. Compared to some years ago our home is a lot louder, full of carefully vocalised praise and levelly expressed remonstration. The baby rolls on a rug, and we cheer; the dog rolls on her tummy, and we whoop; the baby reaches, squawking, for too-hot porridge so we intone gentle warnings, while the dog surges with a hopeful yelp for infant-bound porridge and we chide her, wheedling apologies. Galvanising, consuming, exhausting. When we do find time together we often slip into a grateful silence.

It is a loving thing, and a privileged thing, simply to be able to *sit* with another in companionable wordlessness. Bryher is excellent at this. I could learn a lot from Bryher about just how much of actually important communication – whether about dogs, of dogs, or in relationships – can be conducted without recourse to words.

With a vocabulary of pricked ears and dynamo tail-swipes, how might a *wordless* dog give an account of itself, if not the WOOFS and YIPS that featured in my son's picture books? I learn that in Albanian, dogs 'say' *ham ham*, and in Welsh they proffer a vowelless *wff wff*. The word *dog* itself even presents a mystery, with its etymological roots unknown. Certainly some of the most vivid portraits of dogs have no requirement for words. Chopin features as a character in one of Nell's books, and the inspiration for his 'Minute Waltz' apparently came as he observed a small dog chase its tail; in visual art the skittering dachshund in Giacomo Balla's painting *Dynamism of a Dog on a Leash* (1912) conveys more about that dog's ankle-height propulsion and character than any novel-length exposition could ever hope to describe.

I think of Bryher at her most outraged staccato when I'm dawdling and she wants to smell a compelling lamp post, or her insistent barrelling against my legs if she wants to get under a duvet, and it's clear that a sort of grammar and punctuation is at a dog's disposal. There's an anecdote in Alice B. Toklas's autobiography that offers a neat insight into a form of barkless semantic patterning styled out by Basket II, the (non-)standard poodle with whom she and Gertrude Stein lived: '[Stein] says that listening to the rhythm of his water drinking made her recognise the difference between sentences and paragraphs, that paragraphs are emotional and sentences are not.' As I write this paragraph, I can hear Nell in the other room throwing a ball for Bryher, and explaining to our son why he should leave her so-silky ears alone.

How might Bryher narrate her time with us, or her relationship to what goes on around her?

There have been a number of incredible fiction and non-fiction books that feature authors mediating their dog-subjects' imagined command of a verbal/textual language, communicating canine experiences of the world. We might read Eileen Myles's *Afterglow: A Dog Memoir* (2018) and its account of the poet's deceased pit bull Rosie – 'a masculine girl, British like an old upper-class dyke' – all narrated with doggone wit, waggish relish and stubbornness. Elsewhere in Virginia Woolf's *Flush: A Biography* (1933) social satire and streams of consciousness reveal that language, of course, has always been an unstable, mutable or often insensible commodity anyway. Although I suspect our apparently cheerfully dunderheaded, hearing-aid-guzzling dog would perhaps not have the eponymous Flush's emotional range and sensibilities ('at last he lay still in tense and silent agony' is not a line I can imagine applying to Bryher's life or psychology too often), we detect a clear evocation of a dog's affinities and character through Woolf's writing; a portrait of a dog, and its individuality.

In terms of vocabulary, as much as we might try and teach our dog commands it is definitely true that, without realising it, we have adopted many of Bryher's noises and harrumphs into our day-to-day communication: I find myself mirroring Bryher's startled whinnies of indignation fairly often, or realising halfway through the performance of a querying head-tilt that I have learned the action from the best wet-nosed, long-eared head-tilter in the business. Is this a blurring of lines, or an incorporation of different types of communications and intimacies? Returning to Virginia Woolf, she not only enjoyed the company of dogs throughout her life but often in correspondence she evidently refers to herself and others in specifically dog-terms or guises. In 1927 Vita Sackville-West wrote to her lover, 'I am Virginia's good puppy, beating my tail on the floor, responsive to a kind pat' while almost a decade later Woolf refers to Sackville-West in this way: 'Oh dear, you are a generous, golden hearted woman, dog, or whatever it may be.' We see this again with another queer writer of the last century, the author after whom Bryher is named; she raised a daughter with the poet Hilda Doolittle, and would sign her letters to HD 'with love and barks' and the nickname 'Fido', sometimes also supplying a doodled line drawing of a chirpy terrier on the page.

What is it to identify as or with dogs like this, in terms of love? Do we rely on the canine figure in our idioms or nicknames, in metaphor or for poetic metamorphosis, because of dogs' cultural connotations with mischief, or boundless hunger? Is it the capacity for affection that we associate with them, or their fidelity? Their perceived randiness, their postures of beseechment, or their ability to be trained; do we identify with them because of their warning nips as much as for their lusty barks? All the above, perhaps: both the apparent capacity for boundless affection ascribed to them, as well as their fussy partiality.

Truth be told, I suspect I'd do better to learn how to adopt our dog's uncalculated spluttering, clatter-shuffle genre of narration than attempt to define it in terms of my own. There is a line from Gertrude Stein's work *Identity: A Poem* that is oft-quoted, perhaps as much about love as much as self-knowledge, or wordless dogs: 'I am I because my little dog knows me.'

Love can be a complex stewardship, or a treat, or an objection; it can be mischievous thing, or a pining time; it can be tossing a ball, or finishing a trailing-off of sentences; it can be unabashed, toothy, goofy, guarded, noble; overconfident, swaggering, simpering; love can be no words for half an hour, while sitting dull-eyed at the end of the day, or hand-feeding kibble from a ridiculous saucer, or holding a small teething sleepless shape for hours and rubbing his back; it can be glossy, and unreprimandable; rumbling, and snaffling, and *wff.* It is not an easy command to learn, but sometimes it might be the easiest one in the world.

It's been a year since our son was born,——

——and he is saying his first words. He says 'bye bye', and 'all done', but mostly he says the names of animals: 'cat' and 'duck' and, more often than anything else, 'dog'. He applies the term fairly liberally to all dogs but also to goats, horses and deer. His world is full of dogs, and he delights in them.

Life has taken on a new rhythm, now: the old, familiar rhythm of the dog walk, and the new, chaotic rhythms of the baby's bathtime, reading together, putting him to bed. Often, once the baby is asleep, once Eley and I have collapsed on the sofa, too tired to say much, Bryher flumps her whole weight into our laps, her haunch on one of us and her head resting on her paws on the thighs of the other.

I often think about her puppyhood, when, to help with her recall, Eley and I stood at opposite ends of a small enclosed area in the local park (called, of all things, the Philosopher's Garden) and took turns calling Bryher's name. She ran between us, black and white and frenzied, tail heli-coptering behind her, and as soon as she arrived the other one would summon her away. Our son is currently learning to walk, and I noticed this morning that we assumed the same positions, kneeling on opposite sides of the rug, arms outstretched as we coaxed him to totter between us. It strikes me now that this is the defining image of what it has been like to build a family with Eley: we have less time, we get so much less sleep, but even when we're standing on opposite sides of the field, there are these bright streaks running between us, connecting and complicating and communicating and communing and astonishing us, all the time, moment by moment.

Sovereignty

Carl Phillips

The last dog I owned, or – more humanely put, so
I'm told – that I used to live with, she'd follow me
everywhere. She died eventually. I put her down's
more the truth. It *is* the truth. And now
                this dog – that
I mostly call Sovereignty, both for how sovereignty,
like fascination, can be overrated, and for how long it's
taken me, just to half-understand that.

                           ('Musculature', 1–8)

My dog's name is Ben. After reading this poem
to an audience, I'm always quick to point this out,
since who would be so obnoxious as to name a
dog Sovereignty, I ask them, which always gets a
good laugh. But then why call him Sovereignty in

a poem? Sure, I go on to give a sort of reason, the kind of reason that maybe makes sense within a poem's dream logic. But how did the name occur to me in the first place?

Dogs don't really 'stand for' anything; we impose meaning *upon* them, much as we impose emotions on them that they most likely aren't feeling, not at the time, and not in the ways we understand and experience that emotion ourselves. Likewise, I tend to mean literally what I say in a poem; the literal can turn out, though, to be an alternative way of speaking about another truth, one that's been withheld from the poem, but is just as literal. It is true, for example, that before Ben I owned – lived with – another dog, who did indeed follow me everywhere, and eventually died – I had her put down. But this morning it occurs to me that I adopted that dog with my then partner; that the partner could be said to be similarly dependent on me; that the relationship died – ended; that I ended the relationship of almost eighteen years; that, metaphysically, I put that relationship down.

Ben is the first dog I ever adopted on my own. I did so when, at fifty-three, I was living by myself for the first time in my adult life. On the face of it, I'm pretty sure I adopted him out of habit: I've always had dogs in my life, I've learned to rely on their companionship. But one of the first things I realised when I brought Ben home was that I'd at last have a chance to train a dog as I chose, without having to argue with someone else about whether dogs should or shouldn't be allowed to descend a staircase in front of their humans (why shouldn't they be?), whether a dog should be allowed on the furniture or not (of course they should!), the sorts of things my partner and I had butted heads about often, all of it an unconvincing cover for the realer problems of our relationship: control, judgement, the inevitable fallout of resentment and anger . . . Now *I* made the rules, within and around which I could live without being judged, because who was there to judge me?

'No man is an island,' says Donne, but he also says, elsewhere, 'I am a little world made cunningly,' which has always felt to me like a declaration of self-containment, of the self being enough for a world to consist of. A world that requires only itself is free to do as it wishes – is this not sovereignty? A sovereignty is a self-governing state or can be the authority that allows for self-governance. Sovereignty's ultimately what I'd arrived at, what I'd arranged for myself: no other humans around, just me living alone with Ben, who became part of the household over which I held sway. From there, it's not that much of a leap to translate Ben into a projection of my new-found independence, and to call him Sovereignty as confirmation.

I wrote my poem over six years ago, and only now do I see what I've just pointed out. The poem doesn't go on to be at all about power or independence, yet I wrote it from the context of my new life, and in calling Ben 'Sovereignty' I was acknowledging, and to some extent celebrating, that new life, but privately – by a word that wouldn't reveal to a reader any of what I've discussed and, indeed, wouldn't reveal it to me either, until now. Ben, what have you been up to?

*

I've said for years that poems are like advance bulletins from the interior, by which I mean that our poems often become the place where we express what we're not ready to hear, in language that, in a sense, disguises and delivers that for-now-unacceptable information from and to ourselves. In my own poems, I've found that animals generally, but dogs in particular, often end up being windows into my own psychology. As if the dog were an extension of myself. And indeed while it's fairly proverbial that people seem to choose dogs that resemble themselves physically – a willowy youth walking a greyhound, a short stocky person driving with a muscley little Boston terrier in the passenger seat – I think we're drawn, as with other people, towards dogs whose sensibility aligns with our own. Not that the dog is a mirror of my interior; more like a pond whose surface can be a mirror.

> Released, she seems for a moment as if
> some part of me that, almost
>
> I wouldn't mind
> understanding better
>
> ('White Dog', 8–11)

There's all the rest, below the surface is how I put it once, writing of another dog – the same dog, in fact, whom I mentioned earlier, who used to follow me everywhere. I shared a life with that dog – Andy – for twelve years, until she got too sick and I had to have her put down. Four days later, with mixed feelings of betrayal and a belief that the point of a life is to keep living while we still can, I adopted a black and tan coonhound, who came with the name they'd given him at the shelter: Ben.

Ben was a year old when I adopted him – housebroken, but not yet trained to walk on a leash, or to not jump on people, or to not put two paws on a kitchen counter and eat whatever was sitting there. In my previous relationship, there'd been an insistence on official obedience training, consistency in how we handled the dog – and that wouldn't have necessarily been wrong, but it doesn't fit with who I am. Free to do as I wished, I began training Ben in an organic way: we would find our own rhythms together, naturally, but without compromising the need for some rules, for both our sakes. I spent a year walking Ben on a very short leash, forcing him to stay at my side, after I'd seen how he loved to jump wildly onto any person we encountered, let alone his habit of racing after squirrels and nearly pulling me down if my attention drifted . . . But after that year, once I felt that he'd got my pace of walking, and that he understood it was wrong to jump on people, I put him on an extension leash. He didn't pull at all, and pretty much kept pace with me, as if not entirely aware that this leash gave him more freedom. What he did do, though, is constantly – but unpredictably – weave to either side of the path in front of us. Is this the correct way for a dog to walk? Not according to actual dog trainers. But Ben's walking pattern reminds me of how my own sentences proceed: instinctively, with statements that double back on and revise themselves in the interest of accuracy, with plenty of suspended clauses, a way of holding many possibilities up to the light at once. Divagatory. Digressive. When I first started showing my poems to people, I was told the sentences were too fraught, overwrought – 'too Mandarin,' one teacher told me, which I had to look up and go through several definitions for before I got to Merriam-Webster's 'marked by polished ornate complexity of language.' What, I wondered, can be wrong with that?

What is wrong, likewise, with a dog weaving back and forth as I walk him? Yes, it means I have to retract the leash when we encounter others, to give them room to pass. And yes, it has also meant having to anticipate these weavings, so as not to trip over Ben as he crosses my path. But I've come to see this as a dance that enacts our symbiosis, our natural give and take; it's true that I'm the one who has to accommodate Ben in this regard, but I rather like how that means pushing the usual hierarchy of human over dog towards something more flexible, more fluid.

> The wild dog in my head
>
> that I keep for company, that I'd been told could
> not be tamed, which is why I wanted him, I think
> or I think so now, becomes daily more tractable . . .
> ('Delicately, Slow, the World Comes Back', 6–9)

There's Ben again, this time masquerading as 'the wild dog in my head'. Reading this passage now, I see that I'm partly talking about Ben, though nobody ever told me he couldn't be tamed; rather, I'd been told, most of my life, that I seemed untameable, determined not to conform to expectations – in a relationship, in how I look and speak, and at the level of my sentence-making. As if I were *drawn* to the untamed life, instead of simply living that life, not by choice, but by definition: this is who I am. Of course there's a need for rules, and of course a dog has to learn at least some basic ones, in order to live safely among humans. But who says the goal has to be total submission and obedience? What about restlessness? What about wilderness?

> Half of me says I'm
> the wrong answer, while the other says no, maybe
> just more difficult, the harder one
>
> to choose.
> ('Delicately, Slow, the World Comes Back', 10–13)

I adopted Ben from a shelter here in St Louis. While he'd obviously lived among people at some point – given that he was housebroken – he'd been found as a stray in a decidedly tough part of a still sometimes rough-around-the-edges city. He was calm enough during our meeting at the shelter, but shelter behaviour is an unreliable gauge of how a dog will behave once out of the shelter. Meanwhile, he calmly leapt into the car and curled up on the back seat. 'You've done this before, haven't you?' I recall turning to say to him, though he said nothing back.

But it took only twenty-four hours for the other side to emerge. Not just the jumping on people, raiding the kitchen counters and trying to eat the leash rather than be led by it, but an especially disturbing habit of growling viciously at me, teeth bared, the moment I sat down to a computer, something I tend to do a lot. I'd lived, in an earlier life, with a dog (this was Max) whose aggression never entirely went away – he'd bitten me, he'd chewed the window frames, he'd lost teeth when trying to chew through the back gate to attack a passer-by in the alley. Never again, I'd promised myself. Would I have to return Ben and look for a better match?

Part of why I was determined not to is that when he was good, he was excellent. I could also tell he was frightened by a new environment, and with a stranger; this seemed reasonable. There's a part I've left out, though. Shortly after having left the eighteen-year relationship I mentioned earlier, I entered a period – in the name of freedom – of increasing recklessness, morally, sexually, emotionally. It had led me to those lines about being perhaps 'the wrong answer', but then I'd remember the rest of it: 'maybe just more difficult, the harder one / to choose.' That could as easily describe Ben as myself. We were both frightened. And we could both use a bit of discipline, which is finally maybe less about rules than structure, around and within which rules exist but with a flexibility that can allow them at first to feel like, and then become, a choice.

*

Wilderness isn't wildness. 'If wild, I was once / more gentle.' There's a wilderness inside me I wouldn't live without. Couldn't. A blue heron lifts from the surface of the algae-ed pond Ben and I have stopped beside. Not wild, I say aloud – to Ben, to the heron, as if they could either of them under-stand me – not wild, merely free. Some speak of breaking an animal when they mean they tamed it. Some call it gentling. Somewhere the poet Stanley Kunitz speaks of wilderness as that part of a poem that might make no sense, but without it the poem itself loses meaning. That part of a poem, or that part of a life? I'll break your heart. Break mine.

*

Ben and I have just finished the first leg of a two-day drive from Missouri to Massachusetts. After a day of steady fog and rain and terrible visibility, we've stopped at a hotel roughly where Ohio blurs into

West Virginia. I've done this drive many times over the past twenty years, but never before without another person to share the driving with. I'm sixty-two now. And Ben is eleven or, if what I grew up believing still holds, seventy-seven in human years. Instead of leaping into the car, he now puts his front paws on the back seat and waits for me to lift his rear carriage until he's safely aboard. He clears his throat a lot in the early morning, like an old man, I think to myself, until I stop and realise I tend to do this, too.

I didn't have to do this drive without another driver. I wanted two weeks out east, and my partner (of nearly nine years now) only has a week off, so he'll fly out and join us later. But it's also true that I wanted to 'prove' to myself I could do this alone. And maybe also – or maybe the main reason is – I wanted to do this with Ben, just the two of us. I don't know how many years he's got left, but my track record with dogs is they make it, at most, to thirteen. Ben's from the Midwest, he's barely known the sea, I want him to know it, that particular wilderness that I come from, that after almost thirty years in St Louis has never left me. And I suppose, too, I wanted a brief return to how it used to be, Ben and I together, our own little world, its weather governed by rules we've settled on, over time, between us.

And yet there's none of the recklessness that marked that earlier period when Ben first entered my life. Restlessness, yes; that never leaves – there'd be no longing, otherwise, no desire; so, no imagination. But not recklessness. If I don't exactly fear death, I care about it, I no longer look at it with detachment: death is real, a thing we carry inside us until we don't, the wilderness of ourselves a small one finally, inside a larger one. And because of how Ben has, over the years, been both a lens through which I understand myself better and a guide I've looked to, to redirect and steady me, if only because living with a dog brings pattern and routine and responsibility to a human life, it's hard for me to watch him ageing, weakening, and not remember: we're dying, both of us.

But we were always dying.

But we're not dead yet.

Through the hotel window I can see it's pouring, still. But the room we've got is cosy enough, and the bed's a good one. Ben's snoring quietly, curled up at the end of it, while I read the memoirs of a French aristocrat who lived in the years before and during and after Napoleon's power had dwindled down to nothing. Sovereignty sleeps hard beside me. I pass my hands down the full length of him, like a loose command through a summer garden.

Child-Friendly

Ned Beauman

Here are some facts about me. I'm a single man in my thirties who goes on regular solo trips to Thailand. But when I'm not in Thailand, I spend several hours a week hanging around in local parks with an adorable dog who's an absolute magnet for little girls.

However, I am not a paedophile. I have no way of proving that to you, but I go to Thailand for the food, and I have this dog because . . . well, yeah, OK, why *do* I have this dog who looks like he could have been engineered in a lab to melt the hearts of pre-teens? Tiny enough to put even the most skittish at ease, with a beaming smile like a *Paw Patrol* character and lustrous hair like a fairy-tale prince. Eager to play with everyone he meets and almost flirtatious in the way he seems to sense a child's comfort level and then mischievously walk that line.

Why would a guy like me get a dog like that unless he had some kind of . . . agenda? Especially considering the rest of my personal aesthetic is not exactly *kawaii*. I like brutalism and dystopia, miserabilist philosophy and severe black clothes. By rights I should have some kind of alien-looking sighthound with dusk-grey fur who flits around in a goatskin cape and maybe a Ballardian leg brace. Not this ridiculous little macaroon who would probably get turned down for a supporting role in a Hello Kitty cartoon for being too cute.

Well, it was partly intentional. I just like adorable dogs, OK? But it was also partly unintentional. I didn't realise that Naska, my four-year-old Havanese, would be so tiny. I planned to get a small-to-medium-size dog, and the mistake I made was that I had never knowingly met a Havanese before I threw in my lot with Naska. Which might sound reckless, but it wasn't my fault: in 2017, while I was still making my mind up, I went to an event called Discover Dogs at ExCeL London, which had ambassadors from practically every dog breed on the planet . . .

except the Havanese, whose stall was empty because they hadn't turned up. Maybe they'd heard I was coming and they were scared I might hug one of them to death. So I relied on the internet, and that can be risky: we've all heard about people who get what they think is an incredible eBay bargain on a vintage credenza and when it arrives it turns out to be a piece of dollhouse furniture.

Which is a bit like what happened to me. When I brought Naska home from the breeder at eight weeks old, he was, to quote my next-door neighbour, 'the size of a potato'. And in a sense he still is. He did get bigger. Just not very much. For a while I wondered if there could be something wrong with him, but he's now just under five kilos, which is within the normal range for Havaneses, just on the lower end. In 2011, Peter Glazebrook of Nottinghamshire won the Guinness World Record for a potato weighing 4.98 kg. Yes, that was an unusually large specimen, but nevertheless I have to accept that my dog never definitively outgrew potatoes.

I often refer to Naska as 'the most microscopic object in the universe' or 'the smallest living organism'. Which is unfair, because the truth is he's not even excessively small for a toy dog. He's bigger than a Chihuahua or a Yorkie or a Brussels griffon. So why is it that he *seems* so little? I think it's because he has the physiology of a much bigger dog. People often remark on this. He resembles a rough collie who's been hit by a shrink ray. He looks intrinsically not-to-scale. You simply cannot take him in without thinking 'Why is that dog so small?' (Obviously I ask him this all the time in private but he's never given me a satisfactory answer.)

His size does have certain practical advantages. I can bring him wherever I want because he's so easy to carry around; sometimes I almost forget I'm holding him, like when you're looking for your phone and then realise it's already in your other hand. I can sneak him in practically anywhere when he's camouflaged against my overcoat, and if I ever got caught I could probably just insist he was a hookworm or a louse or some other variety of epidermal parasite. Which is not that far from the truth.

But it has practical disadvantages too. He can slip without difficulty through iron railings; I wouldn't be entirely surprised if he could slip through chicken wire. When we're on a busy street, I worry that he'll get stepped on; when he ventures too far into a hedgerow, I worry he'll get mugged by a couple of tough dormice; and when we're at home, because he can literally fall between the sofa cushions, I worry that one day I'll lose him down there like a 20p coin.

Then there's the issue of LD_{50}, which is a scientific term referring to the number of milligrams of poison per kilogram of body mass that will kill 50 per cent of test subjects. The lower the body mass, the less poison it takes, and Naska's body mass is so very low. Yes, all dogs have to be kept away from chocolate, but Naska is slight enough that if someone scratches his ears and then I find out they've used cocoa-butter hand lotion any time in the past decade I have to rush him immediately to the vet in case it's already overwhelmed his kidneys. Also, his size seriously restricts the range of other dogs he can play with. Which is a shame, because he's an enthusiastic, some might say demonic, tussler. The lightest weight class in mixed martial arts is called atomweight. Even in dog terms, Naska is several notches below that – quarkweight or hadronweight – and it's a lonely place to be for a potential champion who just wants a fair match-up.

But none of this is as insidious as the fear that my motivations for getting Naska in the first place could be called into question. Every time I bring him to the park, I'm neurotic about being misconstrued, about people looking at Naska and thinking he's some kind of unwitting accomplice. I suppose what I have is a meta-paranoia, a paranoia about other people being paranoid. This was probably seeded during my formative years. The early 2000s, when I was a teenager, were the peak of the paedophile hysteria in the UK.

Things aren't quite as febrile today, though this mindset is still with us. A few years ago I was at a folk festival on Tooting Common when my friend's toddler started spontaneously taking all her clothes off, as was her habit at that time. A community support officer bustled over and demanded that the child should be covered up immediately. My friend said, 'Well, she really doesn't seem to want to put her clothes back on, so why does it matter?' The community support officer gestured at the cheerful summer scene and said 'There could be a paedophile!'

Maybe I should just chill out. I don't want to come across like those executives who say things like 'Unfortunately since #MeToo I can't even go to Pret with female colleagues any more in case I'm accused of persistent groping by multiple witnesses.' But I know I'm not completely crazy to worry about this! *The Happy Puppy Handbook* has a section about how to get your new dog used to kids in which the author specifically warns that 'Men have to use some common sense when talking to other people's children. Make sure that the parents are aware and happy that their kids are talking to you and stroking your dog.' And a 2010 survey by the charity Play England found that '44 per cent of men would be concerned to approach a child who needed assistance in their local neighbourhood because people might think they were trying to abduct them.'

Also, I feel like I fit the profile of a paedophile, with my shabby parka, my loner vibe, and above all my undeniably bait-like animal, who might as well be giving out free ice cream. Whenever a child in a park starts talking to me about my dog, all I can focus on is not looking like I'm grooming them. But I also don't want to sour the child's meeting with Naska, because the first time a person meets Naska is in many ways the most important moment of their entire life.

So I end up trying to seem detached without being unfriendly, or nice without being warm, and the end result is a kind of awkward, shifty, self-conscious demeanour which, by disastrous coincidence, precisely mirrors how I behave around an adult woman if I'm intimidated by her extraordinary beauty. No wonder I often find myself rehearsing conversations in my head: 'Look, this is actually the closest park to my flat, and the only reason I come here when it's full of kids is because I work until lunchtime and then by the time I get myself organised to take Naska for a walk it's often three or four in the afternoon, and it's not my fault if that also happens to be when primary schools let out . . .' (By this point I'm imagining myself being chased into an attic like Peter Lorre in *M*.)

In a sense, my fear here is just an intensification of what one feels in practically all social interactions with strangers: what does this person think of me, how am I coming across, are all my worst features on display? For the most part, Naska has eased this for me. When I meet a new person, I basically just thrust Naska in their face, and from then on all I have to think is 'what does this person think of Naska' (they love him and would die for him), 'how is Naska coming across' (dazzling, messianic, epochal), 'are Naska's worst features on display' (not applicable, he doesn't have any).

But although Naska does make social situations easier, in some ways he just throws all my failings into sharper relief. When I'm going around with him, the contrast between us is so stark that it's as if I've attached myself to some improbably glamorous spouse: people look at us together and think 'What on earth does Naska see in him? The man is dead weight!' Naska is delighted to meet any man, woman or child, anyone, literally anyone, simply because they are a person he hasn't met yet. This he has in common with many dogs and a certain set of humans. It's an amazing quality to have, and the humans who have it often do very well in life. Unfortunately, you can't fake it. Well, if you take the right pill, you can experience being a dog, in the sense that for three or four hours nothing makes you happier than running up to a stranger and getting a scratch behind the ears. But it always wears off by the morning.

Still, I hope that just a tiny bit of Naska's personality will rub off on me as the years pass. Of course I'll never match his confidence; you won't see me on a summer's day hopping from picnic to picnic like an old-school restaurant owner working the room. ('Happy birthday! Wonderful to see you! Enjoying your chicken? Can I have some?')

But maybe he can at least teach me how to move through the world with openness and optimism, just as he has already taught me so many things, like how true friendship can transcend species boundaries, and the best places to find fresh human excrement in north London parks. Like I said, there's probably nothing that makes me look more like a paedophile more than my nervousness about being mistaken for a paedophile, so if I can just overcome that, I will have nothing holding me back. As Naska frolics with some little tyke by the swings, I will look her father full in the eye and tell him he needn't worry because the only thing I'm interested in grooming is the silken hair of my exquisite Havanese.

The Harbour

Nina Mingya Powles

Toby whined and howled for most of the six-hour
drive from Taranaki to Wellington. I was sixteen.
We'd returned from Shanghai six months earlier,
where we'd lived for three years. With no more
overseas job contracts on the horizon for either of
my parents, my dad and I had convinced my mum
that it was finally time. Mum was reluctant; for her,
dogs were guard dogs, not pets. *What about the mess,
the smell, and what about when we go away?* But she
gave in eventually, perhaps beginning to sense that
now, finally, there was a chance that this city by
the sea could become our home. I didn't always
know what 'home' meant. Home was a feeling
that changed shape and colour like an ocean

wave. What if it became a real place – somewhere familiar? A harbour: a place to seek shelter, a place to return.

I twisted around in the back seat and looked at the puppy pleadingly, worried my parents now immediately regretted their decision. I wondered how something so small and so fuzzy could emit such a terrible noise. But he wore himself out in the last hour of the drive – a soft brown lump half-hidden in a pile of blankets, lolling side to side as we wove around the coastal road. He slept despite the movement and the noise of waves crashing on the shore. The tide here swept in broad, flat curves, with nothing to slow its course along the slabs of volcanic rock. From the car I could see the speed and force of the undertow, dragging kelp and strings of mussel shells back out. Salt spray and wind whistled against the car windows. I loved the dark volcanic sand of this coastline where I'd been taken on trips when I was little. I loved the way the wind blew here, hard and fast, unlike anywhere else I had lived. In autumn in New York the wind blew fallen leaves in quick spirals. And Shanghai felt like a strangely wind-less city, especially in May and June, when the air became heavy and wet. Here, in Wellington, there was nothing to stop the wind and nowhere to hide from it.

Nine-week-old Toby fit in my lap, though his paws already seemed too big for the rest of his body. 'He'll be a big one,' people said when they stopped to coo over him, which happened every few paces whenever we took him outside. Early on, he was a big dreamer. His eyelids twitched and his paws whirred, sprinting through the fields of his action-packed dreams. Every now and then a string of soft *woofs* erupted, and he startled himself awake. Now I wonder if he was already dreaming of the sea.

*

Jackie, the only dog in my family before Toby, was friends with no one but Gong Gong. I learned this the hard way, reaching out to pet her tail one day – fluffy and grey, so soft, with wispy tufts of white at the tip – and she snarled at me. Jackie was a small dog but I was small, too, and I ran away in tears. I remember her white pointed teeth.

For families who live in large gated houses on the outskirts of cities in Malaysia, guard dogs aren't uncommon. Jackie was a medium-sized cattle dog mix of some sort, with sparkly black eyes and a coat of speckled black and grey, and patches of honey-coloured fur around her belly. She slept outside at night, though she dozed inside all day next to the armchair where Gong Gong had his afternoon nap. Whenever my parents brought me to visit my grandparents, she and I eyed each other suspiciously from across the room. Eventually, over the first few days of each visit, we grew used to each other's presence. I watched her, admiring her lovely black-pepper fur, wishing so badly that she might change her mind and want to be my friend, too. She watched me with one eye shut and one eye open, curled up underneath Gong Gong's chair.

As she got older, and as my cousins and I got older, too, something in her began to soften. She didn't mind so much when my toe accidentally prodded her under the table, or when I brushed past her to get to the kitchen. The softness of her fur on my skin was a small thrill after all those years. She let us sit near her in the shade under the awning overlooking the backyard, where we ate dried peas and practised tossing them into each other's cups. Together we eyed the tall grass for signs of lizards, geckos and white egrets. Dark swallows looped in the air above us at dusk, nesting in a corner of the ceiling above the carport.

Jackie didn't like me much, but I thought of myself as the kind of girl who really ought to have a dog – a sidekick. As an only child, I grew up surrounded by a host of imaginary dogs in lieu of siblings. There was a lineage of dogs from the past that were talked about so much that sometimes I felt like I knew them, and they knew me: Joe, Dad's old Great Dane from when he was little, who slobbered on visitors and whom Dad once tried to ride like a pony; Tasi and Lua, a pair of Labradors beloved by Dad's mum when the family lived in Samoa. Balto the husky was my first fictional best friend, followed by Blue of *Blue's Clues* fame, and Wishbone the Jack Russell detective who solved mysteries of ancient history.

In my eyes, dogs were for families who stayed put. Families who had lived in the same house in the same town their whole lives; not us, who moved countries every few years, taking our belongings with us everywhere we went. I thought of the girls at my school with golden retrievers and cocker spaniels who knew exactly where they belonged in the world, whose families did not look like mine. For them, home did not seem complicated.

I was not as different from my classmates as I thought I was at fifteen, when I'd just left my friends behind in Shanghai, and Wellington felt like the smallest, saddest place in the world. We all went to the same school, lived in affluent suburbs of the city, and our parents did similar government jobs. And if they hadn't met my mum, they often didn't know I was Malaysian Chinese. But I felt different. I wondered what it felt like to have generations of your family all living in the same place. I wondered what it felt like to speak the same language as your grandmother, to be able to tell her about your day and ask her about hers.

*

The classic Labrador traits seem exaggerated in Toby: stubborn, overexcited, food-obsessed, too big and bouncy for anyone to adequately control. We tried puppy school, advanced obedience classes and two different at-home training experts. Jane, the lead trainer at puppy school, wore combat boots with leopard-print leggings, a pouch of treats belted around her waist. Jane had deep respect for the entire canine species but held human beings in pure disdain. Her power over dogs and owners alike was palpable. Conversation ceased when she entered the room. We all waited, straining to listen to her words, terrified.

When it was our turn to demonstrate, Dad made jokes to ease the tension, which made Jane scowl. But in her presence, Toby became a different dog – one we had never met before. His eyes went wide; his whole body quivered with intense concentration. I'd drop his lead and turn away, telling him to stay, and he always did, watching calmly, waiting for my signal.

But not much of this work translated into real life anywhere outside the walls of the school gymnasium in Lower Hutt. Dad dutifully practised commands on Toby's walks, and Toby proved himself capable until any one of his neighbourhood enemies appeared in the distance as a black-and-white blur on the horizon where the walkway curves around towards the shore. At that point, all you could do was hold on for dear life. They never did anything to him that we can remember, but Toby was always deeply suspicious of black-and-white dogs. There was a springy young collie he disliked strongly, barking at her as she came close, but when her owner approached, he fell quiet, rolled onto his back and blinked, waiting for a belly rub.

Once, on the way out the garden gate, Dad noticed that Toby had picked up a dead fledgling.

It was a starling or a blackbird. Dad retrieved it from Toby's gentle mouth, wincing. But the dog hadn't swallowed or chewed it – simply held it gently, walking a few paces with his head down until he'd been discovered. The tiny creature looked as if it were asleep. Retrievers, of course, were bred for their soft mouths, so they could hold the bodies of small prey in their jaws without crushing them.

In 2013, I'd been living in Wellington for four years: the longest I'd lived in any one place since I was seven. Toby was becoming calmer, more mature – a little less bouncy. A few days after the Seddon earthquake that caused damage across Te Waipounamu, the South Island, I was sitting at the dining table studying for my uni exams when an aftershock rolled through. I had heard it coming half a second earlier, a low rumble in the distance. Sometimes you hear an earthquake before you feel it, when the wave of pressure caused by the tremor travels faster than the tremor itself. There was the familiar sound of my mum's china pots tinkling against the window panes, the ceiling lights swinging in slow circles. The carpet pulsed beneath me and I ducked under the table, urgently calling out to Toby, who was napping in the corner in the room. Woken not by the quake but by the sound of his name, he looked up and padded over to me slowly, still half-asleep. We sat huddled together as the gentle shaking slowed to nothing, no more rattling, no sound except our breathing and the wind.

*

I keep leaving. I've left twice since Toby became our dog. After seven years I left to study in Shanghai, then came back, then left again, this time for London. Each departure is brutal, but I do it by choice. I am the daughter of a migrant, but in my adulthood I've become one by choice, not out of any real necessity. Each time, after a period of intense homesickness – which is a kind of grief – I remind myself that I'm the one heartbroken, not Toby, because like all Labradors he will always be content in the company of just about anyone, and I'm only one of his family of four. I remind myself that my leaving is not a hurtful thing, and that I'm always coming back.

In November, visiting home from London, I unclip Toby's red lead and he sprints down the rocky shore to hurl himself into the waves, resembling a seal more than a dog. 'Don't forget to check for orcas,' we used to tell each other jokingly, as one of us followed Toby down the garden park towards the beach. It *is* a joke, mostly: we know the orca only come once or twice a year. And Aotearoa's resident orca population are known to feed almost exclusively on stingrays, not seals, as Antarctic orca do. He becomes a blurry brown shape in the tide, bobbing for sticks, diving under and popping up again a few yards away. I scan the water for shadows and disturbances on its surface. I heap my clothes and shoes on top of my towel, sheltered next to a trunk of driftwood, and wade in after Toby who barely notices, sticks being his main point of focus.

A coarse wind and light rain mixed with sea spray blows in our faces.

The shape and colour of open water is different to the harbour's bays and inlets, where waves sway in soft peaks. Depending on the hour: dark jade, gunmetal, anthracite. The wind blows sideways and the tide shifts direction invisibly. The cold is sharp and quick and I grit my teeth, remembering to breathe, remembering that this body of water is on the brink of summer. In the coming months, while I'm back in the northern hemisphere, stronger sunlight will slowly warm the harbour. The wind will quieten and, on clear days, the surface will turn a blinding shade of blue. To the north of me, factories and industrial plants will continue spilling waste into Te Awa Kairangi, the Hutt River, which flows out into this harbour, endangering swimmers and all who depend on the *moana*.

I swim out towards Toby and back again, cataloguing all the swimming creatures of the harbour both visible and invisible to me: diving seabirds, stingrays, jellyfish, fur seals, *kororā*, whales (orca, humpbacks, occasionally a lone tohorā, a southern right whale) and countless happy dogs like mine. I am part of the harbour and the harbour is a part of me.

After almost a decade back in Wellington, my mum accepted a new job in Beijing – the city where my parents had met. They packed up our old house; Toby went to live temporarily with close friends of ours, who would look after him for three years until Mum and Dad returned. I joined a Facebook group called Cetacean Spotting New Zealand and sent posts every now and then to my parents. A mother orca and her calf gliding past Seatoun Wharf, past Mākaro Island, the backdrop a near-perfect match to the rectangle of sea outside our living-room window. Every time, I thought of Toby. When I was a kid, Wellington always felt like the quiet place in between. It's become that again: an image on my phone's home screen of a pebbly beach and a dark brown dog with a red collar looking out towards the sea, away from me, with the blue hills in the distance, caught in time. We each missed home in different ways. Emails, pictures, texts and hyperlinks were our way of remembering the harbour. Our home, our sea-loving dog.

*

Toby moves more slowly now, stepping tenderly over driftwood and uneven stones. At twelve, he still holds firm to the notion that his walk is not yet over if he hasn't been for a swim. I'm back in

Aotearoa for eight weeks, the first two spent in a quarantine hotel. Once released, I visit Toby as much as I can, walking and swimming and sitting with him in the cool grass under the feijoa tree. His other family, as I've started calling them, are renting out my parents' house, so Toby's day-to-day life looks much the same, just with a different set of humans. It's late summer, unusually warm; the vet said that the cold water likely soothes his painful joints. He can no longer sprint, but still he plods determinedly along the beach. Together, we pick up a new version of an old ritual: I walk headlong into the wind and he follows me towards the shore, keeping up as best he can. We reach the tide and he wanders straight into the sea, just deep enough so that the waves wash over his back but where he can still stand. His feet must know instinctively, as mine do, the place about two metres out where the sand shelf drops off and the shallows give way to deeper water. If you take one step too far, you need to hold your breath before you slip under. But he knows where to stop and he stays there, not swimming, just splashing his nose in the waves, looking out across the harbour at the gulls and the clouds and the twin islands that rise out of the sea ahead of us, so close we could almost swim out to them.

Great White Death

Evie Wyld

Mark a circle in the dirt for my dog.

She made her own circles, sprinting around and around in the leaf mulch while we stopped in the forest and looked for mushrooms. Speedy was a bad dog – part shark, part witch – and it shows in the dreams I have of her, she spins around me through the woods in Parkhurst, her tongue rolling out, her body expanding and contracting with the sound of a galloping horse. My girl was with me from when I turned nine until I was twenty-five, in those soft years when you don't know yourself, but you're trying hard to be something.

She was the runt, which maybe explains her giant appetite; scooped underfed from a concrete cell in the RSPCA on the Isle of Wight. She was like a hare, not a dog, you could see her heart beating against her ribs, fast, you could hear it if you put your hand on her. On the journey home, like a snake she tucked her head down my sleeve and I could feel her eyeballs twitching with anxiety. The same way mine twitched at night with the lights out, the same feeling of no control and no understanding of how to be in the world. Like Speedy I ate whole loaves of bread, stole butter out of the fridge as a child, insatiable hunger for the brief calm that satiation brought. Volume important to us both.

You had to be clear with Speedy though, what was for eating and what was not – she would attempt to consume anything. The stickleback from the bottom of my net, the £20 note in my father's wallet, a tube of laxatives, a nutmeg-sized lump of hash.

Speedy landed us at the vets often with her pancreas: a rib roast pulled from where it rested on the table and dragged off into the woods; a pound of butter fossicked out of a not-properly-closed fridge; the fat of the ham that had been put to the side for a moment, while the meat was cut.

On the Isle of Wight while we camped in the woods, Speedy would take her old hairy companion Panda – a fat Tibetan terrier with a personality disorder we loudly excused because her mother had tried to eat her at birth – off on midnight adventures. They'd go across the main road and then five miles down to New Town, through the woods and over fields, chasing night hares. They'd return to my calling mother, Speedy forty-five minutes ahead of Panda, exhausted; Panda a miracle, dragging brambles and burrs in her hair. Speedy would sleep all the next day in the sun or under a duvet, waking to drink gallons of water and sometimes to vomit up the small bones of some animal she had encountered. Panda nearly died every time, but every time she toddled off along behind the fast dog.

Speedy could take up a double bed with her legs. She would spread out her toes like she had taken off her stilettos and finally her feet could breathe. On cold nights she would burrow into the bottom of my sleeping bag, tangle her legs with my feet, she fit around me like a pair of heated bed socks filled with sticks. Wasps also found the foot of my sleeping bag a nice warm place and if they encountered the dog, she would eat them with her front teeth, crunch them up and let the wings be sneezed away into dust. In this way she guarded me.

She would start panting at about three in the morning when it all became too suffocating down there. She would then stand up in a panic and lurch about the caravan, so that I'd be dragged about by the foot of my sleeping bag, until I could reach down to the zipper and let her poke her nose out. There are few things in my physical memory so strong as the feeling of Speedy nudging under a blanket or into my sleeping bag with her snout, slinking down the side of my body, or if there was space, laying spine to spine with me in the dark.

She was not a badly behaved dog so much as she was badly parented. She was what my mother called *biddable*, she would come – if she wanted to. But she also distrusted most men, especially if they were wearing overalls. If a man came to look at the boiler, she would sneak up behind him and nip the back of his knee. If a man bent down to stroke her and let his face get too close to hers, she'd bite him on the nose. It was never too vicious a bite, it more had the feel of a very upper-class woman slapping away the hand of an urchin who was trying to touch her fur stole.

One time in Wales she found a father and son on a beach who had caught a large fish. They were having a break from fishing and playing football. She scared the boy, took his ball and left it in the shallows, and while his father ran to collect it, she ate the live fish they were keeping in a bucket then sped off down the beach, and like bad dog owners we pretended not to know her until we were out of sight.

The dogs we've had since Speedy have been careful-footed creatures, they for the most part have a sensitivity to their bodies, they don't want to get stung by a nettle or a wasp, or walk on ground that is too rough or hot or cold or prickly. Our current dog Scout will stand on a chair if there is a spilled drink on the floor, even if it is nowhere near her. Speedy on the other hand would charge after prey regardless of the consequence to her physical safety. As a result she had a metal plate in her shoulder, bald bits along her flank where she'd left chunks of herself on fences and barbed wire when she'd turned a corner too tightly. Her pads were so regularly sliced open the scars left prints in the sand. Once, her pink underbelly was undone when she leapt too streamlined over a fence. By the time she was twelve her face was like a shark's, a part of her nose and a part of one ear gone to a red squirrel, slices and a near miss under her eye, the whole face criss-crossed with dark scars.

When I was a teenager and regularly cut parts of myself as a distraction from some of the feelings on the inside of me, she would come and sit next to me, snuffle out the scabs on my legs and arms and she would eat them, and then lick at the places they had been. At the time, I believed this was my dog's bedside manner, her offering me comfort and wanting to fix the mistakes I'd made. Now, having a little distance from it, I do wonder if she was just tasting me.

Speaking of teenage years, Speedy will find your used tampons, she will display them about the house for all to see, eat some of them like mice, she will also dismantle your worn underwear, crotch first, and bring the remains to the guest at the door to welcome them in. She will in old age engage in sapphic pleasures with the new young dog, Juno, who is also that way inclined, but they only do it – they wait to do it – when my grand-mother is visiting. Granny whose understanding of lesbianism aligns somewhat with Queen Victoria's. *What are those animals up to?*

Speedy once dug up a long-buried sausage and placed it as a gift under the neatly tucked and starched covers of the guest bed my grandmother was to sleep in.

My hands remember her face just as my spine remembers her body. I know the temperature of her ears, the two brown dots on the nape of her neck that felt like my own fingerprints. The surprising plumpness of her cheeks and their whisker-lump warts. The foul odour of her breath – no dog has managed to smell as bad – though her teeth were healthy enough, never not chewing in a waking moment. The ragged clip of her front teeth if she felt that I needed defleaing and what a privilege that was, so much of an honour to feel her concern for you and your flea problem that you bore as long as you could, even when she accidentally pinched the skin.

The dog was my introduction to death. I watched her crunch her way through a nest of baby rabbits, saw her cannibalise a fox cub, swallow a shrew whole. She didn't mean anything by it. She was the universe and she was indifferent, she was the great white death of the Isle of Wight and of Peckham Rye Park. I worried about her meeting the Isle of Wight puma, but I wonder who would have eaten who.

She was also the dog who taught me about limitations – my selfishness in keeping her for so long. There were six months at the end she could have done without. Her dog dementia and blindness meant she wandered the house looking for food, eating things that weren't food – pencils, paper bags, fingers that might be sausages. My mother and I took her on one last shaky walk in Battersea Park – the first park she had walked through in London, scared by a bird as a puppy and again as a dying old thing. Between the two walks she had taken her revenge on the scary birds by eating a good number of them.

At the vet's, my first time having a hand in the death of one of our own, the vet quickly and efficiently stopped her heart just as she wolfed down a handful of kibble and she was gone before the biscuits made it down her throat.

I spent the time, then, making sure my hands remembered the feel of her, the ribs no longer vibrating with the scared heart, the blood no longer pulsing behind her ears. But still the soft shell of her, the cold velvet and the feel of her teeth underneath her lips, the odd perturbance of what we called her head bone and the deep icing sugar softness of her throat.

The vet sent her remains to us in a joke coffin with her name in brass on the front. My mum heard groans coming from that small coffin. My father was irritated because he had gone through a mad period of saying he wanted to have her stuffed because she was *such a good animal to look at.* I would have been pleased to have her metal shoulder on the mantlepiece, or a small vial of her bad breath to wear around my neck.

In the end what I was left with for a long time was the space next to me in bed where my body still felt her – she was in the grain of my skin. She still lives in my hands. I can conjure up her warty cheek and the tendon bone of her leg, the serrated pads of her feet. When I first stroked the sole of my newborn son's foot, I thought of her white throat. Had I given birth to a daughter I would have insisted on her taking the middle name Speedy, and then I would have called her by her middle name only. Perhaps luckily for unborn Speedy Wyld we stopped at one boy.

I wonder how I will parent my son without Speedy as a spirit guide – our dog Scout is a wonderful thing but she knows nothing about wild living. She is part lizard, part wombat. They lie together on the sofa, read each other's minds, but both of them keep safe, keep warm and comfortable. Scout has to be pried off the sofa to go to the park, hides when it's time to do anything, likes sliced cheese out of the packet and sits neatly for it, takes it gently from your fingers.

When finally I took the tiny coffin and scattered Speedy on the Isle of Wight in a secret spot, the same place my father is now, I felt such an urge to be mindful of some kind of witchy higher power. There's a small animal graveyard me and my brother dug when we were very young, each shallow grave had a headstone of half a brick and something written there in chalk in case everyone forgot the wounded pigeon who nearly made it but got eaten by the Tibetan terrier, or the shrew clipped in half by the lawn mower, the mole dried on the farmer's fence. Now all those headstones are gone, into the earth, deep under layers of soil and leaves and rotten wood.

I muttered things under my breath as I threw bits of her (or in all likelihood, several unknown dachshunds) into the grass and dirt and in particular at the base of a tree she liked the shade of. I drew a circle in the dirt for my dog, like it symbolised something, though I didn't know what – all I know is that I did the same for my father when I dealt with his ashes and it felt correct and it felt like how things in the wild ought to be treated. Now they season the earth there.

About the Contributors

Ned Beauman was born in London in 1985 and grew up with a Cavalier King Charles called Sasha. The author of five novels, most recently *Venomous Lumpsucker*, he was selected as one of the Best of Young British Novelists by *Granta*.

Rowan Hisayo Buchanan is the author of *Harmless Like You* and *Starling Days*. She is the editor of the *Go Home!* anthology. Her work has won The Authors' Club First Novel Award and a Betty Trask Award and has been shortlisted for the Costa Novel Award. Her work has been a *New York Times* Editors' Choice, and an *NPR* Great Read. Her short work has appeared in several places including *Granta, Guernica, The*

Atlantic and the *New York Times*. She has received fellowships and residencies from Hedgebrook, Macdowell, Gladstones Library, Kimmel Harding Nelson Center for the Arts and Kundiman. More at rowanhisayo.com Her dog, Azuki, doesn't read but does quite like to sit on a manuscript and preferably shuffle the pages around.

Cal Flyn is an award-winning writer from the Highlands of Scotland. She writes literary non-fiction and long-form journalism. Her latest book, *Islands of Abandonment: Life in the Post-Human Landscape*, is about the ecology and psychology of abandoned places. It won the John Burroughs Medal for natural history writing and was short-listed for other prizes including the Baillie Gifford Prize, Ondaatje Prize and British Academy Book Prize. She was also recently announced the 2021 *Sunday Times* Young Writer of the Year. She lives in the Orkney Islands with her partner Rich and their husky Suka.

Writer, poet and curator **alice hiller** worked as a freelance features journalist during the 1980s, covering popular and youth culture. She published a history of the T-shirt with Ebury Press in 1988.

Her PhD at UCL explored transatlantic travel writing. Her poems and reviews have been widely published, and her debut poetry collection *bird of winter*, was shortlisted for the Forwards and John Pollard Prizes. 'Because rescues go both ways' is dedicated to her dogs – Toby, Feldspar and Ithaca – who have taught her the value of regular walks and waterproof footwear.

Jessica J. Lee is a British-Canadian-Taiwanese author, environmental historian, and winner of the Hilary Weston Writers' Trust Prize for Nonfiction, Boardman Tasker Award for Mountain Literature, Banff Mountain Book Award and RBC Taylor Prize Emerging Writer Award. She is the author of two books of nature writing: *Turning* and *Two Trees Make a Forest*. Jessica is the founding editor of *The Willowherb Review*. She is embarrassed to admit that she named her first dog after a department store – but she was thirteen at the time.

Jessica Pan is a journalist whose work has appeared in the likes of *Guardian Weekend, Stylist, Cut, Lenny Letter* and *Vice*. She previously worked as a TV reporter and magazine editor in Beijing and now lives in London. She is a graduate from Brown

University and is the author of the memoir, *Sorry I'm Late, I Didn't Want to Come: One Introvert's Year of Living Dangerously*. She will be asking the Universe for a big soft brown or black dog with floppy ears and a huge heart very soon.

Chris Pearson is an animal and environmental historian based at the University of Liverpool. He is the author of *Dogopolis: How Dogs and Humans Made Modern New York, London, and Paris* (University of Chicago Press, 2021) and is now writing a book on the history of modern dogs for Profile. He lives in Chester with his family and their Bedlington whippet, Cassie.

Carl Phillips is the author of sixteen books of poetry, most recently *Then the War: And Selected Poems 2007–2020* (Carcanet, 2022). His honours include the Aiken Taylor Award for Modern American Poetry and fellowships from the Guggenheim Foundation, American Academy of Arts and Letters, and Academy of American Poets. Phillips has also written three prose books, most recently *My Trade Is Mystery: Seven Meditations from a Life in Writing* (Yale University Press, 2022). He teaches at Washington University in St. Louis, Missouri.

Nina Mingya Powles is a writer, poet and librarian from Aotearoa, New Zealand. Her debut poetry collection *Magnolia 木蘭* was shortlisted for the 2020 Forward Prize for Best First Book of Poetry, and in 2019 she won the Nan Shepherd Prize for Nature Writing. She is the author of a food memoir, *Tiny Moons,* and a collection of essays, *Small Bodies of Water.* Her first dog was Toby the chocolate Lab. She now lives in London with her partner David, a Scottish fold cat named Otto, and a goldendoodle named Kaya.

Nell Stevens's debut novel, *Briefly, a Delicious Life,* was published in 2022. She is the author of two memoirs, *Bleaker House* and *Mrs Gaskell and Me,* which won the 2019 Somerset Maugham Award. Her writing has been published in the *New York Times, Vogue, Paris Review, New York Review of Books, Guardian, Granta* and elsewhere. Nell is an assistant professor in creative writing at the University of Warwick. She lives in London with her dog Bryher, and her wife and son.

Sharlene Teo is a Singaporean writer based in the UK. She is the winner of the inaugural Deborah Rogers Writers' Award for *Ponti,* her first novel. Her writing has been translated into twelve languages and published in places such as *Granta, McSweeney's* and *Guardian*. She also loves dog-like cats, still misses her childhood dogs and plans to get a dog named Macaroni in the nearish future.

Esmé Weijun Wang is the author of *The Border of Paradise* and *The Collected Schizophrenias*. She received the Whiting Award in 2018 and was named one of the Best of Young American Novelists by *Granta* in 2017. She holds an MFA from the University of Michigan and lives in San Francisco. She has lived with her dog, Daphne, for over a decade, and considers her one of the great loves of her life.

Eley Williams teaches at Royal Holloway, University of London. She is the author of *Attrib. and other Stories* (2017) and the novel *The Liar's Dictionary* (2020), with work anthologised in *The Penguin Book of the Contemporary British Short Story, Liberating the Canon*, and commissioned for broadcast by Radio 4. She is a Fellow of the Royal Society of Literature. She lives in London with her dog Bryher, and her wife and son.

Evie Wyld's first novel, *After the Fire, a Still Small Voice*, won the John Llewellyn Rhys Prize and a Betty Trask Award. In 2013 she was included on *Granta*'s once a decade Best of Young British Novelists list. Her second novel *All the Birds, Singing* won the Miles Franklin Award, the Encore Award and the Jerwood Fiction Uncovered Prize.

In 2015 she published a graphic memoir, *Everything is Teeth*, illustrated by Joe Sumner. Her third novel *The Bass Rock* won the Stella Prize in 2021. She lives in Peckham, south London with her husband, who is a published dog poet; her son; and her lurcher, Scout.

Daunt Books

Founded in 2010, Daunt Books
Publishing grew out of Daunt
Books, independent booksellers
with shops in London and the
south of England. We publish the
finest writing in English and in
translation, from literary fiction
– novels and short stories – to
narrative non-fiction, including
essays and memoirs. Our modern
classics list revives authors whose
work has unjustly fallen out of
print. In 2020 we launched Daunt
Books Originals, an imprint for
bold and inventive new writing.

www.dauntbookspublishing.co.uk